Luis Alonso S
Guillermo Gut

MOSES: HIS MISSION

Biblical meditations

Translated by Dinah Livingstone

 St Paul Publications

Original title: *La misión de Moisés*
© 1989 by Luis Alonso Schökel

Cover illustration: *"Orante"* by Marcello Silvestri

St Paul Publications
Middlegreen, Slough SL3 6BT, United Kingdom

English translation copyright © St Paul Publications 1990

ISBN 085439 345 5

Printed by The Guernsey Press Co. Ltd, Guernsey, C.I.

St Paul Publications is an activity of the priests and brothers of the Society of St Paul who proclaim the Gospel through the media of social communication

Contents

Prologue

I have asked Gregory of Nyssa (334-394) to lend me his prologue to his *Life of Moses* in order to write mine. He has told me he agrees but suggests that I use more of his book. I am moved by his generosity and at the same time I am afraid, when I think of the time gap and the difficulty of his Greek style. Understanding my feelings, he who is now outside time encourages me "judiciously" to modernize his language and style.*

I don't know whether Gregory thinks the modern reader is less intelligent or less familiar with rhetoric; he looks at things so loftily...

The idea attracts me and gives me another fright: how will my incidental meditations stand beside pages of Gregory's classic work? But in case my fear is dictated by vanity, I accept his proposal and go straight into Gregory's prologue, which sounds approximately like this:

At horse races the spectators intent on victory shout to their favourites in the contest, even though the horses are eager to run. From the stands they participate in the race with their eyes, thinking to incite the charioteer to keener effort, at the same time urging the horses on while leaning forward and flailing the air with their outstretched hands instead of with a whip. They do this not because their actions themselves contribute anything to the victory; but in this way, by their good will, they eagerly show in voice and deed their concern for the contestants. I seem to be doing the same thing myself, most valued friend and brother. While you are competing admirably in the divine race along the course of virtue,

*English quotations from Gregory of Nyssa are taken, with modifications to fit those of the present author, from Gregory of Nyssa, *The Life of Moses* translated by Abraham J. Malherbe and Everett Ferguson (Paulist Press, New York 1978).

lightfootedly leaping and straining constantly for the prize of the heavenly calling, I exhort, urge and encourage you vigorously to increase your speed. I do this, not moved to it by some unconsidered impulse, but to humour the delights of a beloved child...

Gregory goes on to offer a modest justification for his work. I shall have to justify the liberties I am taking with his text, less for what I take than what I leave out. With this book I should like the reader to be able to listen in short interludes directly to the voice of tradition modulated by the Fathers of the Church.

I need no further prologue except to commend myself and the reader to Gregory's heavenly protection.

1

The birth of Moses

A meditation on the beginning of Exodus must start with certain characters that demand our attention. Two of these are Pharaoh and a newborn baby, who is given the name of Moses. They are separated by a time difference and linked by a similarity of function.

We are told it is a new Pharaoh.

"Then Joseph died and all his brothers, and all that generation. But the descendants of Israel were fruitful and increased greatly; they multiplied and grew exceedingly strong; so that the land was filled with them. Now there arose a new king over Egypt, who did not know Joseph" (Ex 1:6-8).

The Pharaoh is new and side by side with him a new child enters history. These are the two great novelties in this chapter, in which Pharaoh's pre-eminent figure dominates the foreground. Other characters will intervene in the course of the action. But our meditation begins with the two protagonists.

1. Pharaoh

This Pharaoh marks the beginning of a new dynasty in Egypt. He is not the Pharaoh who distinguished Joseph and appointed him his governor with plenipotentiary powers. This is a new Pharaoh who does not know the country. Saying Pharaoh in Egypt is like the Czar in Russia or the Shah of Persia not very long ago – an absolute monarchy. The king has absolute power and does not have to account for his actions to anybody, except perhaps to his own conscience, which is probably not very scrupulous. The new Pharaoh reviews the political situation in his country, and in the north he finds a non-integrated ethnic group, which arouses his suspicions from the first. They are immigrants whose astonishing population explosion has made them a potentially serious threat to their host country. If they keep up this growth rate they will soon be able to claim power. Or they could ally themselves with foreigners and open the northern frontiers to them; invaders might sweep down the whole country from the north like the mighty Nile flood. As a precaution Pharaoh resorts to violent repressive measures. Today we would speak of reasons of state, invoked for fear or simple convenience. National security takes on a military character. But Pharaoh's first measure was an economic one. It is so radical that it is difficult to discover whether the danger of war came first and the economic aspect second, or vice versa. The immediate effect is the enslavement of this dangerous people. Both in peace time and war time they are obliged to do forced labour in the store cities in the north, working on luxury and functional buildings. Their slavery is a fact. The emigrant people welcomed by the Pharaoh of a former dynasty with friendly hospitality, have become a slave people, work-hands, by the new Pharaoh's order. Thus he also intends to curb their demographic growth by weakening them. But won't this measure bring about an undesirable decrease in the work force? Perhaps we should not expect too much coherence from Pharaoh. The main point here is to give a dramatic picture of the new situation. If we want to be conciliatory we can attribute to Pharaoh a policy of controlling his slaves, without eliminating them. The regime of forced labour begins. Taskmasters are set over them to exploit them as labourers in the building of their store cities, Pithom and Ramses. "But the more they were oppressed, the more they multiplied and the more they spread abroad" (v. 12).

2. The oppressed people

From Pharaoh, the oppressor, we turn to the oppressed people. Twelve illustrious persons with their households have settled in Egypt. After a few generations they have become a numerous people and continue to increase. "They multiplied and grew exceedingly strong so that the land was filled with them" (v. 7). The author stresses the statistical fact: a demo-

10

graphic explosion. But isn't he suggesting the presence of a hidden force supplied by God, fertility, thereby fulfilling the promise made to Abraham: "I will multiply you exceedingly... and you shall be the father of a multitude of nations" (Gen 17: 2-4)? The promise is fulfilled in Egypt silently over several generations. Jacob's family is now a numerous people threatening Pharaoh's empire.

God has come on the scene as the protagonist of this extraordinary fertility. Therefore Pharaoh's repressive measures fail. The oppressed people build new cities and create new families. What is to be done? He resorts to genocide, the systematic elimination of all the boys that are born. Not the girls. Females can go to increase the harems kept by Pharaoh, the princes of his court and rich landowners. Then Pharaoh invents a new measure that he considers cunning and effective.

> Then the king of Egypt said to the Hebrew midwives, "When you serve as midwives to the Hebrew women, and see them upon the birthstool, if it is a son, you shall kill him; but if it is a daughter, she shall live" (vv. 15-16).

This is the situation. Pharaoh acts as protagonist accompanied by an anonymous chorus consisting of an enslaved people. God directs the plot and at this point he is going to introduce the liberator of these slaves.

> But the midwives feared God and did not do as the king of Egypt commanded them, but let the male children live. So the king of Egypt called the midwives, and said to them, "Why have you done this, and let the male children live?" The midwives said to Pharaoh, "Because the Hebrew women are not like the Egyptian women; for they are vigorous and are delivered before the midwife comes to them." So God dealt well with the midwives; and the people multiplied and grew very strong. And because the midwives feared God he gave them families. Then Pharaoh commanded all his people, "Every son that is born to the Hebrews you shall cast into the Nile, but you shall let every daughter live" (vv. 17-22).

11

If the women will not collaborate in his extermination plans, then let the men carry out Pharaoh's orders and cut off this people's threatening fertility at birth.

Now another character or group of characters come on stage and their role will increase in the second chapter. Playing a fundamental role in these two chapters on the birth of Moses are the women.

3. The women

It is natural that women should play an important part in birth. Motherhood requires it. Although the physiological ideas of the time wrongly limited the women's contribution to reproduction, there can be no doubt that when a child is born into the world, for much of its care for a long time, women are more important than men.

But the context here is also the birth of liberation. We are about to celebrate the birth of the people of Israel in Egypt, and women are also actively present at the various stages of this birth. First we have the group of midwives; two of them have names, the rest are anonymous. They received an order and it was dangerous to resist or disobey Pharaoh's orders. But they did resist the order, they faced the danger and did not kill the babies. Why? The text says that they "feared God". We may add that these midwives were involved at life's wonderful and mysterious beginnings. Every life that comes into this world comes out of a mother's womb into the hands of motherly women. This contact with helpless new life seeking to enter the world and see the light of day, gives the midwives a religious respect for life and the God of life. For these women fearing God does not consist in offering sacrifices or in praying devoutly. It means facing political dangers and saving innocent lives. The midwife is a woman who collaborates with the mother in bringing the new life into the world. These midwives are brave and ironically astute. When Pharaoh's police inquire why they do not kill the baby boys, they reply with calculated cunning: "We don't do anything. We help the mother, we go to her house and when we get there everything is over. The Hebrew women are strong and have amazing power in labour." And they smile secretly at their clever answer and the simple ignorance of Pharaoh's henchmen, who know nothing about these matters and are easily convinced. God rewarded their defence of life with the gift of motherhood.

Another female character is Moses' sister. We should try to "imagine the people, see what they do and hear what they say". Moses is put into a basket and placed on the waters of the Nile. His sister is watching the floating cradle's course from the riverbank. The basket stops in a backwater. So does she. At this moment another woman appears, the princess, one of Pharaoh's many daughters. She is bathing in the Nile under the heat of the Egyptian sun. She has her ladies-in-waiting with her to protect her at a distance. The princess sees the strange object floating on the water, whirling about until it stops among some reeds. She orders her ladies to go and see what it is.

> The daughter of Pharaoh came down to bathe at the river, and her maidens walked beside the river; she saw the basket among the reeds and sent her maidens to fetch it. When she opened it she saw the child; and lo, the babe was crying. She took pity on him and said, "This is one of the Hebrews' children" (vv. 5-7).

She is the second female character. She is diverted in her bathing and curious. The basket is light, made of wicker perhaps, well plugged underneath, partially closed on top. They open it expectantly and are surprised by the crying child. The princess is moved. Pharaoh feels no pity in giving the extermination order, neither do the soldiers and guards when they see it is carried out. But the princess, as a woman, feels pity when she sees the crying child. She is firmly for life. Even though it is a Hebrew baby it still has a right to live. Her maternal instinct does not understand reasons of state invoked by Pharaoh's men. For her the right to life is more important. She takes pity on him and says, "This is one of the Hebrews' children."

Hiding among the reeds on the river brink, the baby's sister also tries to defend life. No one asked her to do it and she runs a great risk. In spite of the prohibition, she is spying on Pharaoh's daughter while she is bathing. The risk does not bother her. She sees the princess's reaction, perhaps a tear on her cheek. She

13

hears her words – we must suppose that she understands the Egyptian language – and she pre-empts any questions by feigning generosity: "Shall I go and call you a nurse from the Hebrew women to nurse the child for you?" She does not say a nurse that will just "nurse" the child, but one who will "nurse the child for you". Because she foresees that the princess will take the child and adopt it in some way.

> And Pharaoh's daughter said to her, "Go." So the girl went and called the child's mother. And Pharaoh's daughter said to her, "Take this child away, and nurse him for me and I will give you your wages." So the woman took the child and nursed him. And the child grew and she brought him to Pharaoh's daughter, and he became her son; and she named him Moses [Hebrew: *Mosheh*], for she said, "Because I drew him out [Hebrew: *mashah*] of the water" (vv. 7-10).

The third female figure is the mother. She becomes nurse to her own child. She is going to nurse him for the Egyptian princess, but at least nurse him herself. The midwives, the mother, the sister and the princess join as links in a chain protecting the child, they form a ring of tenderness, which Pharaoh's power cannot enter. They are all women.

4. God

The most important character still has not come on stage. Where is God in this story? It appears that all the initiative is taken by humans: Pharaoh, the princess, the mother, the sister, the midwives. God is directing the action secretly, through the people's prodigious fertility and the midwives who fear God. He is the subject of all the action, even though grammatically he appears to act in apposition to the named subject. The midwives fear God because he has revealed himself to them in the birth of many new lives; he has opened the eyes of their minds to see that life is a gift of God. God worked on their minds and they responded in their behaviour. God organises the course of events, because they are involved in the birth of Moses, the people's leader and liberator, God's lieutenant. The whole story

14

of oppression and the different scenes converge towards this event, which I have called "the birth of the people of Israel in Egypt". I use the word in a Christian sense, because Moses is the figure and type of Christ. Hence the importance of his birth. We are not going into the problem of the legendary character; we are simply commenting on a text. God dominates events. For him "a thousand years in thy sight are but as yesterday when it is past, or as a watch in the night" (Ps 90:4). If God had ordained Moses' birth twenty or thirty years earlier, the liberator would have been present and ready at the beginning of Pharaoh's oppression. But, in the Exodus story, God waits, allows a whole generation to grow up and suffer, lets events run their course, and when the moment comes, he does not send a liberator prepared for the task, but a child. He will have to grow up and mature slowly through difficulties. When the time is ripe, a moment determined by God himself and not the stars, the liberator is born. And when the fullness of time comes, our own true and universal liberator will be born. Why not before? It is for God and not us to determine the historical moment and the way in which he intervenes. "At the set time which I appoint I will judge with equity" (Ps 75:2). It is not his style to intervene in history with spectacular miracles, which he keeps for exceptional occasions. His policy for governing the world consists in taking the strands of history to plait a coloured cord running through it. Events succeed as he wishes, even though we may call them ironies of history. Sometimes there is a 180 degree turn, a "revolution", and everything flows towards the point he wants. Pharaoh uses drastic repressive measures and everything turns out the opposite to what he intended: the people increase, in spite of the forced labour, the midwives cleverly trick him; and his own daughter is the one who saves the providential child, born of a Hebrew woman, to become the liberator of the enslaved people. Even the Nile appears to be in complicity, carrying the fragile wicker basket to a backwater where the princess comes to bathe. The ironies of history are really strings pulled by Providence. There was a need for Pharaoh's cruelty, the mother's desperation, the sister's curiosity, the dangerous river journey in the basket, in order for the princess to take pity on the child. These prodigious events converge providentially towards a liberation project desired by God.

The Israelites read the story of the birth and early life of their great leader with pride. In a broader perspective we can grasp that the future liberator must experience the liberation story personally, in advance. One of the events in this story is the passage of the Red Sea, victory over the waters, the arrival on the opposite shore via the dry waterbed. The child Moses is given up to the Nile's fierce current and conquers the water. Threatening water becomes liberating water. Moses set free prefigures Moses the liberator, his birth prefigures the Saviour's birth, when God's clock strikes the fullness of time.

5. Moses' early activity

A new chapter, shorter and less important, tells us about Moses' early activity. The event ends in a wedding but the wedding is not the happy ending of a story written to entertain its readers. Everything remains in suspense. Moses takes charge of his own life and Pharaoh's daughter retreats into the background. Her task of giving her adopted child an education at court is over. Moses has become a young man responsible for himself, he is familiar with the Egyptian language, its customs and culture. He is accepted and recognized, and he can remain as a high-up official because of his talents and qualities. In modern terms, we would say that Moses can make a career at Pharaoh's court. The fact of having been adopted by the princess allows him to rub shoulders with other princes of the royal blood and he for his part has assimilated what is best in this culture. Religion? The text tells us nothing, but we know that Moses does not accept the Egyptian religion. Neither does it appear to be required of him.

In the second chapter of Exodus, without any reference to Moses' age we are simply told: "One day when Moses had grown up, he went out to his people and looked on their burdens". He leaves the court because the voice of his blood urges him to go and find his fellow Israelites. He has been adopted by the princess, but his siblings are neither her subsequent children, nor cousins or other princes and princesses educated at court, children or grandchildren of Pharaoh. No. His brothers and sisters are the Hebrews, the oppressed and enslaved people, whereas the Egyptians are the oppressors. He shows solidarity with the suffering of the Hebrews, whom he feels are his brothers. This is the context in which the first active episode in Moses' life is set.

He saw an Egyptian beating a Hebrew, one of his people. He looked this way and that, and seeing no one he killed the Egyptian and hid him in the sand.

When he went out the next day, behold, two Hebrews were struggling together; and he said to the man that did the wrong, "Why do you strike your fellow?" He answered, "Who made you a prince and judge over us? Do you mean to kill me as you killed the Egyptian?" Then Moses was afraid, and thought, "Surely the thing is known" (vv.11-14).

His blood boils. He is indignant and cannot tolerate that an Egyptian overseer should beat a poor Hebrew. He comes so violently to the defence of his Hebrew brother that he kills the Egyptian, having first looked round to see that no one is watching. The police might have been around. With all his strength – perhaps with a weapon – but chiefly with his indignation, he comes to the defence of justice, in solidarity with his Hebrew brother. He brings the matter to a close by burying the corpse and going away.

The action seems noble to us. But did he need to kill the Egyptian? Separating the contenders would have had graver consequences because the Egyptian would have denounced him. By killing him he gets rid of ill-treater and witness, because there are no other witnesses. So Moses thinks, but he has committed a violent deed and therefore a dangerous one. He has received no special commission from God. Is violence the way to liberation, is this Moses' mission? Would he be able to eliminate all the Egyptian oppressors one by one? The next day brings us an answer.

This time it is not an Egyptian ill-treating a Hebrew. This time two Hebrews are fighting each other. It means that selfishness is not just structural. Not all Egyptians are bad or all Hebrews good. Selfishness and oppression also exist among the Hebrews. The case of two Hebrews fighting each other is a more difficult proposition for Moses. The two are brothers and he cannot take

17

sides with one against the other. He renounces violence and turns to persuasion. Why are you striking your fellow? It is like saying: Don't you realize our situation? We are suffering oppression and we should stick together and defend ourselves. Your selfishness is stronger than your solidarity. It is not right for you to ill-treat your fellow. The man answered, "Who made you a prince and judge over us?" He does not accept Moses' reasoning. Instead of acknowledging his guilt, he reacts as if he had been publicly humiliated. Instead of surrendering he throws out a challenge, which is also a dangerous threat: "Do you mean to kill me as you killed the Egyptian?" It is as if he were saying: I saw it all, I know what you have done and I can denounce you to the authorities. I know something that can ruin you and be your death.

Moses was afraid because he thought his action was unknown. He thinks the matter is dangerous because the police could get to hear about it. And he thinks there is also an internal danger, perhaps more serious, that his action might provoke the distrust of his own people. The Hebrew is accusing him of being a violent man, capable of murdering in a fit of temper. His Hebrew brother does not trust the violent Moses and this distrust could spread among all the other Hebrews if this one opens his mouth. Moses is afraid. It is fear of his own violence and fear of the Egyptian police. The only solution is to flee. First he fled from the court to go to his brothers. Now he must flee urgently from Egyptian territory. These flights are exoduses [exodus: departure]. And with these departures he is again prefiguring the people's great departure. But on this occasion his departure is a flight.

6. In Sinai

When Pharaoh heard of it, he sought to kill Moses. But Moses fled from Pharaoh, and stayed in the land of Midian; and he sat down by a well. Now the priest of Midian had seven daughters; and they came and drew water, and filled the troughs to water their father's flock. The shepherds came and drove them away; but Moses stood up and helped them, and watered their flock.

When they came to their father Reuel, he said, "How is it that you have come so soon today?"

They said, "An Egyptian delivered us out of the hands of the shepherds, and even drew water for us and watered the flock."

He said to his daughters, "And where is he? Why have you left the man? Call him, that he may eat bread."

And Moses was content to dwell with the man, and he gave Moses his daughter Zipporah. She bore a son and he called his name Gershom; for he said, "I have been a sojourner [Hebrew: *ger*] in a foreign land" (vv. 15-22).

The geography, the scene and the action have changed. Now Moses is a fugitive. He appears to be in the Sinai peninsula and there, near an oasis, he is free and safe. His arrival is marked by his idyllic meeting with a group of girls. It is like a fairy story and, for an Israelite story, the number seven is very appropriate. They are seven sisters but they are not matched by seven brothers. There is only the one stranger. They have come to draw water, a woman's job at that time familiar from the stories of the patriarchs, particularly that of Rebecca. When they are at the drinking troughs some shepherds come to drive them away. Why? They are not intending to abuse them. They are behaving badly because they want to go first. They are strong men and want to impose the law of the strongest. It is a problem of the time. Watering a large flock could take a long time, and they are not prepared to wait that long. They want to go first. The scene has no particular importance. It merely reflects a small abuse of male power claiming arbitrary privileges by force.

Moses witnesses the intended injustice. Neither the girls nor the shepherds are his sisters or brothers. They are unknown foreigners rather than Hebrews or Egyptians. Impetuously he spontaneously sides with the weak. He defends the girls' right of having arrived first. This is not a romantic gesture or a love story. The author stresses Moses' defence of what is right. He gets angry with the shepherds and defends the girls because he considers there has been an abuse of force, which was the reason why he defended his ill-treated brother. The romantic part of the story comes later. For the moment he simply sides with justice, one against many. When they have done their job the girls can go home early with the flock to their father Reuel's house. They explain why they have been so quick, because something unusual has happened; an Egyptian defended them against the shepherds, drew water for them and watered the flock.

The seven sisters' father does some quick mental calculations, not spelt out by the writer but easy to imagine: if this man is a foreigner and comes on his own account, it must be because he has some problem; if he took such an immediate and effective initiative he must be an impetuous character; if he took on several others alone, he must be strong. Strength, decisiveness and a sense of justice for the weak. The worthy father immediately thinks of him as a useful addition to the family business and a good catch for one of his daughters. His mind is made up for practical reasons. History should not necessarily be read as romance.

GREGORY OF NYSSA: THE BIRTH OF MOSES

Moses was born at the time Pharaoh issued the decrees for male offspring to be destroyed. How shall we as a matter of choice imitate this fortuitous birth of Moses? Someone will rightly raise the objection that it does not lie within our power to imitate in our birth that famous birth. But it is not hard to begin the imitation with this seeming difficulty.

Everyone knows that anything placed in a world of change never remains the same but is always passing from one state to another, the alteration always bringing about something better or worse. The narrative is to be understood according to its real intention... Now, it is certainly required that what is subject to change be in a sense always coming to birth. In mutable nature nothing can be observed which is always the same. Being born, in the sense of constantly experiencing change, does not come about as the result of external initiative, as is the case with the birth of the body, which takes place by chance. Such a birth occurs by choice. We are in some manner our own parents giving birth to ourselves by our own free choice in accordance with whatever we wish to be, moulding ourselves to the teaching of virtue or vice.

We can most certainly enter upon a better birth into the realm of light, however much the unwilling tyrant is distressed, and we can be seen with pleasure and be given life by the parents of this goodly offspring, even though it is contrary to the design of the tyrant.

When we lay bare the hidden meaning of the history, Scripture is seen to teach that the birth which distresses the tyrant is the beginning of the virtuous life. I am speaking of that kind of birth in which free will serves as the midwife.

Life of Moses 1-5
PG 44:328

COMMENTARY

In this text of Gregory's we find a method of commenting that we can call psychological and moral. He takes the story on account with its realism, and assumes that under the two-dimensional surface of the text lies a dimension of depth which he calls "enigma", that is, a truth that has to be fathomed. This deep truth is a principle of human conscious and responsible life. In psychological terms it is free choice that creates a new being or way of being for good or evil. That "enigma" veiled in "history" and unveiled in "theory" or contemplation, is proposed as the principle of spiritual life, for which Moses' whole life proves to be exemplary. By this exegetic mechanism Pharaoh is transformed into a personification of the forces of evil which continually oppose the birth of the good, in a struggle as dramatic as the biblical account.

2

The call of Moses

Conventionally we call this meditation "the call of Moses". Among the many callings we read about in the Old Testament that of Moses in Exodus chapters 3 and 4 is the one about which we are given the most information and detail. We can distinguish five important encounters or aspects which constitute the five points of our meditation. The first is God's apparition in the fire; the second the liberation project; then Moses' mission, God's identifying of himself by name and finally the conversation between God and Moses.

1. The burning bush

Now Moses was keeping the flock of his father-in-law, Jethro, the priest of Midian; and he led his flock to the west side of the wilderness, and came to Horeb, the mountain of God. And the angel of the Lord appeared to him in a flame of fire out of the midst of a bush; and he looked, and lo, the bush was burning, yet it was not consumed. And Moses said, "I will turn aside and see this great sight, why the bush is not burnt." When the Lord saw that he turned aside to see, God called to him out of the bush, "Moses, Moses!" and he said, "Here I am." Then he said, "Do not come near; put off your shoes from your feet, for the place on which you are standing is holy ground" (Ex 3:1-5).

The text tells us that the angel of the Lord appeared. We imagine an angel, as it is commonly represented in the iconography of the West, as an intermediate being. We must correct this idea. Here and in many other Old Testament texts, which speak of an apparition, something visible, a perceptible manifestation of God, the writer avoids making God the grammatical subject and interposes the linguistic device of an angel of the Lord, his messenger, his envoy, which could also be interpreted as an apparition of the Lord: the Lord revealing himself. Because later when this messenger of Yahweh speaks, it is the Lord speaking in person. In other words, there are texts in which the angel of the Lord and the Lord himself alternate as the subject. In other texts, apart from rare exceptions, the "angel of the Lord" is used to speak of a manifestation to the senses and "the Lord" is only used when it is he who speaks.

Here we do not have an intermediate or angelic being inferior to God. And because it is a direct manifestation of God we find the Hebrew word *mal' ak* [messenger]. The Lord appears in the fire, actually in a burning bush. When Moses turns aside and draws near or tries to draw near, he observes that it is not the bush which is burning, it is not flames burning the bush, but a fire that has found a place to flare and makes its presence known, not on bare earth or rock as in other texts, but in a bush.

Now we have three elements: the angel, the manifestation in the form of fire in the bush and the Lord. The most significant of these three is the fire. Why does God appear to Moses in a fire and not in a lightning or in a storm? We know that God's most frequent and classic manifestation in the Old Testament is the storm. "Manifestation of God" is what is meant by the Greek word *theophany*. The dominant theophany in the whole of the Old Testament is the storm, the tempest, which in some cases can be a volcano. Here do we have lightning striking the bush? When we speak of lightning we can say that fire fell from heaven. But here nothing is said about anything falling from heaven; it is a flame springing from a bush. A more accurate translation reads: "out of the midst of the bush". It is not a single bush but a patch of bushes, scrub.

Why the fire? Because fire is one of God's elements. All the elements belong to God: water, earth, air... but let us remember that the earth with water and air was given to human beings, whereas the heavens belong to the Lord, and God keeps fire as an element of his presence. From the many texts we could quote, here is Psalm 50:3: "Our God comes, he does not keep silence, before him is a devouring fire". Psalm 97:2-5 is fuller and more explicit:

Clouds and thick darkness are round about him;
   righteousness and justice are the foundation of his throne.
Fire goes before him,
   and burns up his adversaries round about.
His lightnings lighten the world;
   the earth sees and trembles.
The mountains melt like wax before the Lord,
   before the Lord of all the earth.

We could give many more quotations but let us move straight on to consider the dominant aspects of the element *fire*. One is that it is *inaccessible*. "Who could live in a devouring fire?" For God lives in fire and is therefore inaccessible. When he reveals himself on Sinai, it is as if the whole mountain is in flames. The people cannot approach God. If they approach when they should not they will become fuel for the fire. Furthermore fire is God's element and can sometimes be the bringer of his punishment, a punishment which annihilates, destroys and totally consumes.

So on the rough plateau where he is grazing his flock Moses suddenly sees this astonishing flame flaring in a bush and wants to go up to it to see what is going on. But he hears a voice: "Don't come any closer!" The fire is inaccessible. God dwells in the fire and moreover he does not tolerate evil, he has to destroy it, consume it in his devouring fire. But what happens here is that the flames burn, rise and move, roar through the bush without scorching a single branch or leaf. The bush is undamaged. We may imagine that the bush is green. If the flock is going out to graze it is because it can find greenery. The flame moves in the green bush without touching or destroying it. The bush with its thorns also has something inaccessible about it. It is not a domestic plant or a generous fruit tree but a harsh wild bush defending itself with its prickles from man and beast. Divinity is there, inaccessible because of the fire and the thorns. Moses' first meeting with God has something terrible about it. Here he does not behave impulsively as he did with the Egyptian. He is thoughtful and cautious, he thinks something strange is happening, that needs to be observed with care, watching his step. No one can approach fire thoughtlessly and certainly not such a strange fire. Fire can burn useless or harmful plants but with this bush nothing happens.

25

The prophets also make use of this image. All these bushes and thistles are useless vegetation that is in the way, taking up space and nourishment from the earth. So they must be condemned to the fire. Once the scrub has been burnt up, the earth becomes free and fertile to produce good fruit.

As the bush on Sinai is not consumed, it turns into a sign that God has passed there and left it intact, or maybe these green branches have remained marked forever by God's closeness. Who would not be this bush and feel the "flame of living love" that burns but does not consume!

It is Moses' first encounter with the Lord, the angel, the Lord's manifestation. There will be other meetings of the Lord with his people and fire will also play an important part in these, for example, in the great theophany on Sinai. A great storm, with thunder and lightning flashes accompanies the Lord's descent; these elements taken together create the impression of an erupting volcano. In this first meeting between the people and the Lord, the divine manifestation takes the form of fire, and it is as if the divine fire not only touches the mountain to make it smoke, as the psalm says (104:32) but also goes inside the mountain to make it erupt and more fire burst forth from within. The fire is the Lord's inaccessible presence. Later this same fire is tamed and turns into a column of fire lighting up the night to guide God's people. When the people need to camp the column of fire stops on the ground to show them where. This pillar of fire which is permanently fuelled by God leads the people's march and goes ahead to show them the way. It is the same divine fire tamed now to serve the people. But beware! If some guilty ones rebel, give way to ambition and do not accept the mission of Moses, fire from heaven can fall on them and burn them up. This is what happens to Korah, Dathan and Abiram (Num 16). When the people have sinned God withdraws and denies them his presence, because otherwise it would consume them like a devouring fire. God can give light and warmth but respect demands keeping a distance.

2. The liberation project

Continuing with our text we read that God said to Moses:

"I am the God of your father, the God of Abraham, the God of Isaac and the God of Jacob." And Moses hid his face, for he was afraid to look at God.

Then the Lord said: "I have seen the affliction of my people who are in Egypt, and have heard their cry because of their taskmasters; I know their sufferings, and I have come down to deliver them out of the hand of the Egyptians, and to bring them up out of that land to a good and broad land, a land flowing with milk and honey, to the place of the Canaanites, the Hittites, the Amorites, the Perizzites, the Hivites, and the Jebusites. And now, behold the cry of the people of Israel has come to me, and I have seen the oppression with which the Egyptians oppress them. Come, I will send you to Pharaoh that you may bring forth my people, the sons of Israel, out of Egypt" (Ex 3:6-10).

After identifying himself God tells the reason for his visitation. God has not come to visit Moses to engage in a conversation between anchorites. The Lord comes with a very clear liberation project. Liberation from what? It will always be liberation from something evil. God is speaking of his people. So we can speak of a movement that begins with an act of compassion and solidarity. God has seen the affliction of his people, he has heard their cry and knows their sufferings. Seeing, hearing and knowing. God is aware of the vicissitudes in human history. This time Pharaoh is attacking and the Israelites are being attacked. He is a mighty emperor and they are a slave people, working for him to build store cities and sumptuous and luxurious buildings. God knows Pharaoh the oppressor as well as the oppressed people and he listens to their cry. He cares about their sufferings because they are his people, or they are his people because they are oppressed: both versions are found in various texts. It is assumed that from then on the Israelites are God's people.

By this going back to the beginnings of history, when there was just one family in three descending generations (Abraham, Isaac and Jacob), God is saying that the whole present community is God's people, because they are all descended from the patriarch Abraham, to whom God gave the divine promise. Because they are his people, God does not ignore them: God has seen, heard and come down. God's presence is conceived as a descent from above, where people imagined God lived throughout the Old Testament.

Moses is completely bewildered and cannot answer but to reassure him the Lord spontaneously offers him a sign. This is a piece of local information usually to be found in texts like this one. The one most similar is that of Gideon, a poor Israelite who lived in another period of repression, although it was not so fierce. Suddenly the angel of the Lord appears to him – again we have here a play on words: it is an angelic-manifestation when he is visible and the Lord when he speaks – and Gideon immediately states his objection. What can I do when I am nothing, how can I liberate the children of Israel? But God answers: I am with you. Gideon asks: Give me a sign that it is you speaking to me and that you will help me in this task. And God gives him a sign (Judg 6:11ss).

This happens frequently. God may even offer a sign of his own accord, as in the case of Ahaz, who, however refuses it, piously protesting: "Again the Lord spoke to Ahaz, 'Ask a sign of the Lord your God; let it be as deep as Sheol or as high as heaven.' But Ahaz said, 'I will not ask, and I will not put the Lord to the test'" (Is 7:10-12).

This sign-giving, common in stories of calling, has intrigued and disconcerted commentators and readers. "I will be with you; and this shall be the sign for you, that I have sent you: when you have brought forth the people out of Egypt, you shall serve God upon this mountain" (Ex 3:12).

What is unique about this sign? Perhaps two things. First, that it does not consist of any extraordinary action, merely a liturgical act. A liturgical act is not a miracle, and therefore the sign offered has nothing that makes it a sign. What is really strange is the time in which this sign will be given. It is normal for Gideon to ask for a sort of official guarantee of authenticity before accepting the commission, to prove that he is not a victim of his own imagination. And he is given it: See, I will put out this fleece in the night damp; if the dew falls on it and not around it, that is the sign.

This is what God says but still Gideon is not convinced.

Because he thinks the wool attracts and collects dew in a different way from sparse grass or bare earth. And he asks for the proof to be reversed: for the dew to fall all around it and the fleece to remain completely dry. God agrees and that night the sign occurs. Having been given these two signs by God Gideon decides to undertake the task (Judg 6:36-40).

Moses argues the same way: How do I know it is you who is sending me? God replies: You are going to bring the Israelites out and when you have brought them out you will meet here and celebrate a liturgical service. But, thinks Moses, if I have already brought them out, I won't need any sign.

The inconsistency is obvious and his objection is valid. This means we must look closely at the text and clarify what it means.

This liturgical service takes place at the end of one stage and before the beginning of another. At the end of the stage of the coming out of Egypt they will meet on this mountain before beginning the march through the desert. The desert adventure may end well or may lead to dispersal and death. The first stage functions paradoxically: Moses has to accept the mission God entrusts him with, he has to commit himself to the task God imposes on him with faith and confidence. For faith is adhesion to God, adhering or sticking to him. If I have faith in God, God is with me, and this conviction in faith and through faith enables me to act and perform the task. Once it has been done I can look back and say: it is true, it was a mission from God.

The people of Israel, a slave people, can meet on this plateau and rejoice that it was all true: God wanted to free his people. It will be a liturgy of the experience of liberation not a liturgy of an experience of constraint, rules and prohibitions. Thus it was when Peter came out of prison. He walked along the street and when he came to a crossroads at the end of it, he suddenly realized: it was true (Acts 12:8-11). This is the sign God offers Moses: a sign in the future which engages faith in the present. A guarantee after rather than before the event. Moses understands and his objections change course.

3. Moses' mission

When God introduces himself as the God of Abraham, Isaac and Jacob, in a way he is identifying himself. We habitually imagine God on high, in the sky. So in this conventional language we read that God has come down from his throne in the tranquillity of on high because he cannot bear to see his people suffer. He has come down to liberate them from the Egyptians. Liberation will not simply mean taking them out of oppression but he will also create a new freedom for them. This is announced in a refrain: I have come down to bring them out of this land to lead them into a wide and fertile land, a land flowing with milk and honey, the land of the Canaanites... The Israelites will overflow the limits of this narrow land, which will become incapable of containing them, and they will spread into other territories, a wide land where there will be room for all. Forced labour and the precarious life of Egypt will be succeeded by a free life in the abundance of a land flowing with milk and honey. It is true that this land is occupied by various tribes, but God is Lord of all the earth and assigns peoples their territories. He has destined this special land for his chosen people.

This is God's plan. It is not a plan to support the powerful but to liberate the oppressed.

And a strange thing happens. In the text it appears there are two things that contradict each other, do not agree at all. First God says: I have seen, I have heard, I have noticed and therefore I have come down to liberate them from the Egyptians and bring them out of this land. And then to put his decision into effect he adds: Come, I will send you to Pharaoh, that you may bring forth my people. There is a logical gap, an inconsistency in the narrative, a substitution of functions: I have come down to bring them out but I am sending you so that you be the one to bring them out. The predicate does not change: go and bring out, but the subject does change. At first the subject is God, who comes down to liberate them, to bring them out. The second time it is still God who sends but the subject who is to bring them out is Moses. So what does this inconsistency in the narrative really mean? The commentators have tried to explain it in a plausible manner by recourse to two sources or two narrative strands – the Elohist and the Yahwist – the two accounts the author has plaited together resulting in a single plait with two strands. This does not make everything clear or explain everything but it is a plausible, reasonable explanation. It does not explain everything because the result is a new story.

The inconsistency in the narrative has aroused curiosity and excited inquiry. God comes down to free his people but he does not go in person to speak to Pharaoh, taking a form like the one he took on his visit to Abraham (Gn 18:19). His way of coming down and liberating is to send a man and this gives rise to a theological and spiritual theory of *mediation*. A man is sent by God, he has a mission. God comes down because Moses cannot go to Pharaoh on his own account. In a rush of anger and indignation Moses killed an Egyptian. Now Moses is a shepherd, married to a daughter of the priest of Midian, although this fact is not given much importance. The important thing is that now Moses is being sent [Latin *missus*] and he must go and fulfil the mission entrusted to him by God. From this moment he gives himself over to the mission for which he was born and called. The mission is bound up with God's coming down to liberate his people. Nobody should be disconcerted that the story speaks alternately of "God bringing out" or "Moses bringing out". The reader will come to see a sort of game in which the one throws the ball to the other in an alternating "I brought out", "you brought out" the people. It is important to stress this mediating character of the man sent by God. It signifies God's entry into history, becoming human in a special mediation, which is prefiguring another unique entry of God into history, not mediately but fully, without fire or forms, delegates or mediators, but in a real and full humanity, when he really becomes man.

A first objection arises as in all accounts of calling. The chosen one does not usually respond with enthusiasm to his mission. Of course it is an honour, a glory, a privilege to be chosen by God. But there is a mixture of pride and fear: I like it but I do not dare undertake it. It is a double reaction of respect for the task and the one commissioning it, but at the same time a lack of self-confidence. Will I be capable of properly carrying out a command by God, a divine mission? Won't it be too much for me? And this is also Moses' first reaction:

But Moses said to God, "Who am I that I should go to Pharaoh, and bring the sons of Israel out of Egypt?"
God said, "But I am with you" (Ex 3:11-12).

31

Let us pause here. From the human point of view, God "being with you" is a guarantee of success, a strong support. "I am with you" is the plainest phrase imaginable, just a verb, almost on its own, a subject and a simple predicate. Here the wise almighty God is not saying who he *is* but who he *is with*. It's all there. It is not possible to say more with less. What can anyone fear who feels God's presence? He can go with courage and accomplish the most dangerous mission. The same phrase means on God's part: I am the one who will liberate the people but I am going to liberate them by *being with you*. I don't need to supersede you or displace you from history. I am going to come down and free them by being with you. This is the prolific double dimension of a phrase which will be repeated again and again.

4. God's identity

In the call of Moses there appears an extremely important element, God's self-identification, giving his name. When you send an envoy, an ambassador with full power, you have to identify yourself: I, the emperor, send you as my envoy. This identification of the sender is essential to define the mission. Moses has already heard one identification. That God who has appeared to him in the fire, who has begun speaking to him and who categorically sends him to Pharaoh to negotiate the people's liberation, is at least the God of the patriarchs. This is in itself an identification, but as well as this title God needs a name. All the gods have their names by which they are identified, invoked. So Moses asks, rightly: When I go and present myself to the people of Israel on your behalf, whom must I speak of? What name must I give so that they pay attention to me?

> Moses said to God: "If I come to the people of Israel and say to them, 'The God of your fathers has sent me,' and they ask me, 'What is his name?' what shall I say to them?"
> God said to Moses, "I AM WHO I AM." And he said, "Say this to the people of Israel, 'The Lord, the God of your fathers, the God of Abraham, the God of Isaac and the God of Jacob, has sent me to you': this is my name for ever, and thus I am to be remembered throughout all generations" (Ex 3:13-15).

This is a vital text, fundamental to research into the Pentateuch. But here we are in a meditation and this is not the place to engage in scholarly discussion. We must restrict ourselves to getting at the meaning of the name of the one who must identify himself.

He offers two forms of identification, which are the name – in Hebrew it is probably *Yahweh*, for which we know the consonants but are doubtful about the vowels – and the title "God of the patriarchs". These are the identifying data which appear in the text as a play on words. What are you called? I am called "I am who I am". Go and tell the people of Israel: "I am" has sent me to you. And speak to them of "the God of your fathers..."

In order to understand this we must first reflect on a Hebrew custom of interpreting names. Technically it is called *paranomasia*, the art of interpreting names. Here we are not going into academic linguistics, philology or rigorous etymology. We take the name as it immediately sounds and give an explanation, interpreting the name by the sound it produces in the ears of the Israelites. So, the word Yahweh, if we accept these vowels for the consonants, sounds like a jussive form of a causative conjugation of the verb *hyh:* "to be" (which could be a variant of the verb *hyh*: "to live").

Let us take it as it sounds: *haya* = be, and so this sound Yahweh, heard not as a name but a word would sound practically like "make be", which would be the proper name of this mysterious personage. We take the fact of being, existing, and the causative form. But as we have already indicated, the biblical authors are not offering a rigorous etymological explanation such as we are proposing now, but playing freely with the word. This name Yahweh contains the root *hyh*, which means "be". Perhaps the Spanish distinction between *ser* and *estar** can help us understand the Hebrew word play. Moses formulates his first question thus: "What are you called?" God answers: I am (*estoy*) with you, in the first person. I am [*soy*] who am [*estoy*] with you. I am [*soy*] who am [*estoy*] freeing the people of Israel. And later: You will say to them: I Am [*soy*] has sent me to you. Yahweh has sent me... etc.

* Spanish has two verbs meaning "to be": *ser* and *estar*. *Estar* is related to the English "stand" and means to be at, with, etc. In this text *soy* (from *ser*) means "I am" what I am, and *estoy* (from *estar*) means "I am/stand" where I am.

Here the word play is on the fundamental matter of being-existing. The author is not intending a philosophical or metaphysical reflection on the name, but it appears very probable, firstly, that the name was already known, because you can only play with a name that is already known; secondly, that the author discovers in this name the presence of the verb to be/exist and although this does not provide us with a metaphysical definition, this is very significant for us in order to conceive God, imagine, address him, because it sets God radically and fundamentally in the order of being/existing. If we take it in the causative form, then we have *the one who makes be*, whereas if we take it intransitively, we simply get *he who is*. Therefore without going into metaphysics, which in our traditional philosophy would speak of *being of* or *for himself* [*ens a se* in Latin], something radical is still being said in the spontaneous, normal, even colloquial register we have here, as nothing is more radical than being or existing. For everyone can say "I am" but only he can say it in a special and unique way; and when we turn to him he wishes that we should do so at this fundamental level of being or existing.

We must stress that this is a reflection, but it is a reflection arising from the data given to us by an author who has tried to play with the name in which he has heard God's being and existing. As we said, Spanish uses both verbs *ser* and *estar*: "*Soy el que soy*: I am who am," "*Soy el que estoy*": I am who am/stand (where I am)" i.e. "*Soy el que estoy contigo*: I am who am/stand with you". This translates the whole movement perfectly: Yahweh is the one who has sent me. Yahweh, that is, "I am who am", "I am who am/stand (where I am)" is with you. The word play in the Hebrew text is subtle and can serve us for our meditation. We are interested in God's titles but above all in his name, and his name embraces the fundamental of being.

In the second item of information, the titles, God defines himself as the God of the patriarchs. He is not a new divinity, the past has not been abolished but explicitly connected with the present. This establishes the biological continuity: you are the descendants of those patriarchs. There is an unbroken human continuity between Abraham, Isaac, Jacob and yourselves. But this biological continuity, which could be shown in a genealogical tree, now acquires a theological significance: the children of

Abraham are the children of the promise, they are God's word made flesh, God's promise become reality. Therefore recalling the patriarchs is the same thing as recalling the promise: you exist as the promise of "I am", "I exist", because you are the descendants of the promise made to the patriarchs who give existence to a family line thanks to God's special blessing. Thus the perspective of the people's liberation from Egypt is set on a broad horizon, a limitless horizon and becomes a segment of a gigantic arc which began in the time of the patriarchs and will not end with this generation. Because before and afterwards, and above all, it is the Lord who *is* and *is with* Moses, as he was with Abraham and is with his people whom he jealously calls *his*.

This patriarchal title expresses a guarantee: God holds the reins of history, channels time's flow and he can stop, accelerate or go backwards as he likes. He is the Lord of the course of history and his patriarchal titles are a guarantee for us, just as his name is. With it he gives us an important chunk of revelation because he adds: this is and this will be my name for ever, thus you will call me from generation to generation. We continue using this name but we have given a new name to the God of the Israelites in Egypt, the God of Moses and the patriarchs who is also our God. We now withdraw from the articulated sound of this meditation to listen in silence to the name God has for us today. He has some titles and a name, but for us he is the Father of our Lord Jesus Christ and at the same time our Father. He is the same God who freed the Israelites from Egypt, fulfilling his patriarchal promise because he is and always will be himself and he is always with us.

5. *Dialogue between Moses and God: objections and replies*

The main thing has been said but we should also consider Moses' objections and God's answers. We shall treat them as complementary. For there is something that Moses still does not understand and this prevents him fully accepting his mission. He resists and struggles to avoid commitment. He is afraid, he does not feel up to it and he argues with God in a sort of trial of strength like arm-wrestling. He gives reasons against and when God answers one he comes back with another. One objection is that neither Pharaoh nor the Israelites are going to take any notice of him. The Israelites will merely see him as the violent man who had to flee. Without credentials they will not believe him. And if they do not listen to him he cannot make them move by force, because obviously this thing cannot be done by force. So it amounts to a request for credentials.

For us credentials are usually a written and sealed document which guarantees the bearer is an envoy. The word "credentials" comes from the Latin *credentialis* meaning to believe, "give credit". Without credentials Moses will have no credibility, will not be given credit. And he needs the people to believe him in order to carry out his task. At the moment he has no credibility and it is up to God to accredit him. This is his first objection. The second refers to his ineptitude as a speaker.

The credentials God gives Moses are the power to work miracles. First faith was required to engage in the task and only at the end would the sign come to seal its authenticity. Now however, God is prepared to give the Israelites a few precursory signs of a miraculous sort and Moses must in some way assume the functions of a magician or conjurer in competition with Pharaoh's magicians. This superhuman power will give credit to his mission and he will have to exercise it before the astonished eyes of the Israelites in a series of transformations or metamorphoses, which will take place in his shepherd's crook, his leader's hand and the waters of the Nile. The first two have a particular significance, closely connected to his person. For while his crook is a tool of his trade as a shepherd, the hand is the seat and organ of action. The third concerns the Nile which is vital running water and the single artery that sustains Egypt's life. These are the three elements in which Moses' transmuting, miracle-working powers will be displayed.

The first is the shepherd's staff or crook :

> "But behold, they will not believe me or listen to my voice, for they will say, 'The Lord did not appear to you.'" The Lord said to him, "What is that in your hand?" He said, "A rod." And he said, "Cast it on the ground." So he cast it on the ground and it became a serpent and Moses fled from it. But the Lord said to Moses, "Put out your hand, and take it by the

tail" – so he put out his hand and caught it, and it became a rod in his hand – "that they may believe that the Lord, the God of their fathers, the God of Abraham, the God of Isaac and the God of Jacob, has appeared to you." Again the Lord said to him, "Put your hand into your bosom." And he put his hand into his bosom; and when he took it out, behold, his hand was diseased, as white as snow. Then God said, "Put your hand back into your bosom." So he put his hand back into his bosom; and when he took it out, behold, it was restored like the rest of his flesh. "If they will not believe you," God said, "or heed the first sign, they may believe the latter sign. If they will not believe even these two signs, or heed your voice, you shall take some water from the Nile and pour it upon the dry ground; and the water which you shall take from the Nile will become blood on the dry ground" (Ex 4:1-9).

The shepherd's staff is an instrument of office useful to lean on and to walk through passes and gullies. But it can also be used to guide the flock. When a sheep is left behind or separated from the others and the shepherd does not have the help of a faithful dog, his crook is useful to him to encourage, drive and gather the sheep. The crook is firstly for support and secondly to drive the flock and thirdly to protect it. If it is threatened by a harmful animal – a jackal or a wolf – the crook can be used for defence and to drive off the predator; it has various functions.

In the hands of Moses and after its transformation the staff gains a very particular function. It could be called a "magician's rod", even though it is not a thin stylized cane, but a genuine shepherd's crook.

A moment arrives in ancient culture in which the rod becomes a sign of power, authority and changes its name to become a "rod of office" or simply "sceptre": it is in effect the prolongation of the human arm. This is the symbol and seat of power, strength and action. The human arm, which can be raised or lowered, stretched or relaxed, is prolonged in this piece of wood which is the rod office, or sceptre, and also serves to increase the arm's power when directed at a person or object. The sceptre can be grasped and held vertically, in a gesture that affirms authority and it can also be leant against the shoulder. The king can support himself on the sceptre, which is like supporting himself on his own authority and if he raises it this gesture makes clear the exercise of his authority.

The shepherd's rod has become a symbol. Moses' rod will also undergo transformations. Moses has used it in its more direct function to hit with or to support himself. Now God orders him to throw it on the floor without controlling it and it turns into a serpent. What had been vertical and governed by the man becomes autonomous as a menacing reptile. Now it is not Moses holding the sceptre. He has lost the power to grasp it and when he lets it go the sceptre becomes independent and turns into a wild and threatening serpent, which Moses is afraid of and wants to get away from.

But we can imagine God's smile as he says: Don't be afraid, take it by the tail. Moses does so, encouraged by God's words, and the moment he grasps it and takes control of it it turns back into a rod subordinate to human power, not detached in sinuous and menacing form. Henceforth Moses' arm will be prolonged in this rod of office, sceptre of authority and the people and the elements will obey him.

The second miracle consists in the transformation of his hand. The hand is the organ and symbol of action (not necessarily strong action, but skilled action). The word "dexterity" means the skilled capacity of the right hand. We also speak of having a good hand, and in the opposite sense we use left-handed to mean clumsy, "cack-handed". So the hand – usually the right hand – is the symbol and metaphor for controlled action. Moses must now put his open palm into the breast-fold of his tunic, which acts as a purse or pocket. There his hand is not active but rests inert. God orders him to do so and when he does his warm hand becomes paralysed and snow-cold, as in the disease of leucodermia. It has become bloodless, repugnant and lifeless. Moses is frightened of his own hand, but God orders him: Put it back in again. And the hand is restored to its natural state.

Moses' hand is not meant to remain pocketed and inactive, but to guide with skill. With it he will be able to work miracles which will convince the Israelites. And if these are not enough, there is still the last one, the Nile water, the vital life-stream of Egypt which waters the plants and drives the pumps, a source of life in its irrigation, clean for bathing and providing energy to the mills. This water spilt on the ground by Moses turns into blood, spilt lifeless blood.

These are Moses' credentials: power over the elements to work miracles. If the Israelites do not credit the first, they will credit the second and if not that, the third. But they will have to believe.

"I am not eloquent," Moses protests as his second objection. If the hand is the organ of action and the arm the seat of power, the tongue is the organ for speaking and Moses will have to use his tongue when he goes and presents himself before Pharaoh. He will be going to him with a difficult and demanding message. He is going to ask him nothing less than that he should let the Israelites go to a ceremony of worship and he has nothing but words and reasons to convince him. And the Lord himself has made things difficult by warning him that Pharaoh will be stubborn and hard. Moses will need a power of oratory which he lacks.

> But Moses said to the Lord, "Oh, my Lord, I am not eloquent, either heretofore or since thou hast spoken to thy servant; but I am slow of speech and tongue." Then the Lord said to him, "Who has made man's mouth? Who makes him dumb or deaf, or seeing, or blind? Is it not I, the Lord? Now therefore go, and I will be with your mouth and teach you what you shall speak." But he said, "Oh, my Lord, send, I pray, some other person." Then the anger of the Lord was kindled against Moses and he said, "Is there not Aaron, your brother, the Levite? I know that he can speak well; and behold he is coming out to meet you, and when he sees you he will be glad in his heart. And you shall speak to him and put the words in his mouth; and I will be with your mouth and with his mouth, and will teach you what you shall do. He shall speak for you to the people; and he shall be a mouth for you, and you shall be to him as God. And you shall take in your hand this rod, with which you shall do the signs" (Ex 4:10-17).

And in another version we read:

> "I am the Lord; tell Pharaoh king of Egypt all that I say to you." But Moses said to the Lord, "Behold I am of uncircum-

cised lips; how then shall Pharaoh listen to me?" And the Lord said to Moses, "See, I make you as God to Pharaoh; and Aaron your brother shall be your prophet. You shall speak all that I command you; and Aaron your brother shall tell Pharaoh to let the people of Israel go out of his land" (Ex 6:29-30; 7:1-2).

These are the two texts. Moses' objection is reasonable and reasoned: a person who has to negotiate, argue, request, demand, must have all the resources of language at his disposal, for persuasion and oratory. Moses does not have the gift of words, in spite of his life in Pharaoh's court and his special education. What we know about Moses up till now consists more of deeds than of words. We saw him intervene impulsively in the case of the Egyptian. When Jethro's daughters watering their flock were ill-treated by the shepherd, Moses intervened and saved them. Moses is a man who acts almost without speaking. Only the dialogue with God and the specific nature of the mission he is given provoke him to speak up and express his objections: his mission is prophetic and he realizes that a dumb stuttering messenger will not be able to fulfil it worthily.

God replies to his objection categorically: If I gave you a mouth I can also teach you to use it. If I gave you a tongue I can also make it agile, flexible, fluent and convincing. And he adds: I will be in your mouth, which is a variant of "I will be with you". It is equivalent to saying: when you have to speak in my name, I will be there in your mouth, moving it and articulating your words, so that it is not you who are speaking. You will not be a messenger who mechanically repeats his message learnt by heart, or who has learnt its substance and then develops it. In your speaking as in the surging of your thoughts and expression of your arguments, I will be with you, directing your mouth, and you are going to be my word.

Moses' disbelief makes God angry. If you insist, it will be Aaron who speaks. You will tell him the gist, give him instructions and he will be the speaker. And in the second version: You will be like a God to Pharaoh. You will be presented to him as a superhuman being, endowed with superhuman powers. But you will do it in silence, and for communication you will have Aaron as your subordinate who will translate your arcane messages so that Pharaoh can understand them. Therefore you will be like a God and Aaron will be like your prophet.

It is another way of saying the same thing, but the author has succeeded in introducing the figure of Aaron into the story as an intermediary and the text has become rounded out.

We shall end by looking to the future with a brief reflection for all those who receive a mission to speak from God: the word of witness, the word of the Gospel, preaching to exhort or denounce. The way is not through violence but persuasion, because reason communicates in words whereas unreason resorts to blows. Therefore we also need the Lord to be in our mouth. Moses, who is not good at speaking, will have to speak out on many occasions and in many ways, addressing the Israelites to reproach and denounce, addressing God to pray and intercede. And after a long mission in action and words, before he goes up the mountain to die, Moses will attain the height of language, which is poetry and he will compose as his testament the great poem, which the Israelites learn by heart: the Canticle of Moses, to be found in chapter 32 of Deuteronomy.

Moses' calling is to be a prophet. Henceforth he does not take the initiative, he does not proclaim himself to be a liberator, because he receives it all from the Lord and must be entirely at his disposal. This is Moses' calling and mission.

GREGORY OF NYSSA:
THE BURNING BUSH

In the same way we shall live a solitary life, no longer entangled with adversaries or mediating between them, but we shall live among those of like disposition and mind who are fed by us while all the movements of our soul are shepherded like sheep by the will of guiding reason.

It is upon us who continue in this quiet and peaceful course of life that the truth will shine, illuminating the eyes of our soul with its own rays. This truth, which was then manifested by the ineffable and mysterious illumination which came to Moses, is God.

And if the flame by which the soul of the prophet was illuminated was kindled from a thorny bush, even this fact will

not be useless for our inquiry. For if truth is God and truth is light
– the Gospel testifies by these sublime and divine names to the
God who made himself visible to us in the flesh – such guidance
of virtue leads us to know that light which has reached down even
to human nature. Lest one think that the radiance did not come
from a material substance, this light did not shine from some
luminary among the stars but came from an earthly bush and
surpassed the heavenly luminaries in brilliance.

From this we learn also the mystery of the Virgin: the light of
divinity which through birth shone from her into human life did
not consume the burning bush, even as the flower of her virginity
was not withered by giving birth.

That light teaches us what we must do to stand within the rays
of the true light: Sandalled feet cannot ascend that height where
the light of truth is seen, but the dead and earthly covering of
skin, which was placed around our nature at the beginning when
we were found naked because of disobedience to the divine will,
must be removed from the feet of the soul.

Life of Moses 18-22
PG 44:332-33

COMMENTARY

In the fire bursting from a bush and manifesting God's
presence, Gregory sees an image of the incarnation: God bursts
from our earth and makes the Father present. He is contrasted
with a purely heavenly light which could be from the stars. Now
the instrument of the incarnation is Mary, who receives God's
Son as mother, and makes him a son of humanity without
damaging her virginity. A figure of this is the bush which is not
consumed by the fire which burns in it. Finally, the fire is a light
which illuminates, and the human mind must take off its shoes
of dragging human prejudices in order to reach this light.

3

Moses and the spirit

Chapter 11 of the book of Numbers is a complex narrative composition. In this meditation we are interested in the theme of the spirit which is broached in Moses' prayer to God, continues in God's answer to Moses and concludes with a solemn liturgy. But first let us look at the chapter as a whole, beginning with verse 4.

1. Narrative context

The Israelites on the march – the chosen people and also other persons who have joined them – begin to protest because they are sick of this single food, which is manna. The same thing to eat every day! We want a change, and that change to be meat. Moses' reply is not addressed to them but to God, whom he confronts in an admirable prayer, which we will comment on in another meditation on Moses' prayer.

Moses complains to God: I cannot cope with this burden! God's reply to Moses: It's very simple, find some helpers, share the burden and the spirit with them and you will be able to cope.

God replies immediately to the people's impatient demand for meat to eat. He sends them flocks of quails and they eat till they are stuffed and suffered colic for their greed. When this episode is over – the people's protest, the eating, the punishment – we come back to Moses' helpers and enter fully into the theme of the spirit.

Moses possesses God's spirit for his task. Now he will share part of this gift among his helpers. God himself indicates the ritual, which is performed in a liturgical ceremony. The chapter might end here but suddenly an epilogue is added suggesting that the outpouring of the spirit spread beyond the limits originally foreseen.

This is the view of the chapter as a whole, in which two narrative strands are interwoven: the people's protest and eating; and the distribution of the spirit among Moses' assistants. Having clarified this let us approach our theme, the theme of the spirit. We have here God's answer to Moses, who complains that he cannot cope with the whole people by himself and asks for help.

How are we to understand this help? Is he asking for God's help or other people's? It appears that what Moses needs and asks for is help from God. Perhaps to rest from his work of leadership while God himself takes it on. But God indicates in his reply that it will not be himself who takes on the burden. Moses must bear the burden, but yes, he can seek some human assistants to help him bear it.

Here we have two points. The first, the burden, is introduced in chapter 33 of the book of Exodus. The text is so closely linked to what is related here in Numbers 11 that some exegetes would put the passage we are studying narratively and contextually as a follow-on to the first verses of Exodus chapter 33. There we read:

> The Lord said to Moses, "Depart, go up hence, you and the people whom you have brought up out of the land of Egypt, to the land of which I swore to Abraham, Isaac and Jacob, saying, 'To your descendants I will give it.' And I will send an angel before you, and I will drive out the Canaanites, the Amorrites, the Hittites, the Perizzites, the Hivites and the Jebusites. Go up to a land flowing with milk and honey; but I will not go up among you, lest I consume you in the way, for you are a stiff-necked people" (Ex 33:1-3).

Moses must lead the people that he himself brought out of Egypt. He will have an envoy of God's with him, an angel, but God himself will not be a companion on the journey, because he is very demanding: he is like a consuming fire. Moses feels alone without God's definite presence and when this moment comes – in Numbers 11 – he complains to God saying: why do you ill-treat your servant?

The coupling is possible, although not necessary. In Numbers 11 the sequence is also coherent and fluent: the people complain,

Moses does not know what to do and passes the complaint on to God.

2. The "senate"

This is what the distribution of the spirit and the burden is leading up to. We shall call it the group or "college" or "senate" that assists Moses. Such an institution is widespread in Israel and we find it repeated or extended with variations among other peoples, in the Church and civil society. It is a group of competent persons, usually of a respectable age who share in the government with a deliberative vote or determining function. We usually call it a "senate" [from the Latin *senes* = old person] and it is a group of people who are thought to be mature in their judgment because of their age.

The same institution exists in the Old Testament: they are the *zeqenim*, the elders. The word originally means the age, but later becomes the function.

This group of "senators" make their appearance at the very beginning of the Exodus but their most important appearance comes in chapter 18, where Moses receives friendly family advice from his father-in-law Jethro.

> "You and the people will wear yourselves out, for the thing is too heavy for you; you are not able to perform it alone... Choose able men from all the people, such as fear God, men who are trustworthy and who hate a bribe; and place such men over the people as rulers of thousands, of hundreds and of fifties, and of tens... Every great matter they shall bring to you, but any small matter they shall decide themselves; so it will be easier for you, and they will bear the burden with you" (Ex 18:18-22).

Many writers relate this chapter 18 of Exodus with Numbers chapter 11. Later in the great chapter 24 of Exodus, when Moses arrives for the meeting with God, he is accompanied by a "senate", a group of seventy elders who are going personally to visit the Lord. So already in the book of Exodus we have an early vision attesting the existence of this "senate" of Moses' assistants, the "elders".

3. The spirit

So Numbers chapter 11 does not occur in a vacuum. It speaks of a subject with which we are already in some way familiar. But it introduces another new theme: the theme of the spirit.

The spirit is a gift of God. In the Old Testament the Holy Spirit is not yet spoken of as a person of the Trinity: Father, Son and Holy Spirit. The spirit is spoken of as God's energy, that creates, orders, is the motive force of history and moves human beings... it is usually called the spirit of God or the spirit of the Lord. Sometimes it is called the Holy Spirit but not with the force and concentration that this term has for us.

As leader and guide of the people, Moses has a quantity – in quantitative terms – and a concentration of gifts of this spirit in order to fulfil his mission. God, who has given Moses a mission and a burden, endowed him with qualities to carry out his task. These qualities are gifts, capacities, the spirit of God. And if Moses' assistants are going to assume part of the burden entrusted to him, logically they will also receive part of his qualities, his spirit.

We can study and understand this manifestation of the spirit by means of a text whose story occurs much later but which was perhaps written earlier. We refer to an experience of Saul's, the first king of Israel. The prophet Samuel anoints Saul king of Israel. At that moment the king receives the qualities, the necessary spirit for his function. These are manifested in a peculiar manner:

"... After that you shall come to Gibeah of God, where there is a garrison of the Philistines; and there, as you come to the city, you will meet a band of prophets coming down from the high place; headed by harp, tambourine, flute and lyre; they will be in ecstasy. Then the spirit of the Lord will come mightily upon you and you shall prophesy with them and be turned into another man. Now when these signs meet you, do whatever your hand finds to do, for God is with you" (1 Sam 10:5-7).

This frenetic dancing is an orgiastic type of dervish dancing in a trance.

A bit further on we read:

When they came to Gibeah, behold a band of prophets met him; and the spirit of God came mightily upon him and he prophesied among them. And when all who knew him before saw how he prophesied with the prophets, the people said to one another, "What has come over the son of Kish? Is Saul also among the prophets?" (vv. 10-11).

In Israel orgiastic dancing manifests the presence of the spirit, it is one of the functions of the *nebi'im*. In our case Saul possesses the spirit to govern because he has been given the anointing conferred by Samuel on God's behalf. This spirit reveals itself in gestures, incorporating Saul in the orgiastic dancing of the group of dervishes. But Saul does not receive the spirit through contact with the prophets. This contact only shows externally what exists within him.

4. Commentary

Now we have our principal reference points to understand and meditate on a particularly important text. We have placed it in its context. Moses needs help, but divine or human help? God responds by promising him human help.

Human help – the first theme – is the senate, the elders.

The gift of the spirit – the second theme – and its orgiastic manifestation.

With these two elements now it is possible to read the verses of chapter 11 that concern us:
In verse 15 Moses says angrily to the Lord:

"If thou wilt deal thus with me, kill me at once, if I find favour in thy sight, that I may not see my wretchedness".
And the Lord said to Moses, "Gather for me seventy men of the elders of Israel, whom you know to be the elders of the people and officers over them; and bring them to the tent of

meeting, and let them take their stand there with you" (v. 16).

So Moses went out and told the people the words of the Lord; and he gathered seventy men of the elders of the people and placed them round about the tent. Then the Lord came down in the cloud and spoke to him, and took some of the spirit that was upon him and put it upon the seventy elders; and when the spirit rested upon them, they prophesied. But they did so no more (vv. 24-25).

Someone saw a change of subject here, because the spirit makes these men "prophesy", and the Hebrew verb indicates here ecstatic, orgiastic manifestations. This is not what it's about, they say. They did not need the gift of the spirit to prophesy, but the gift of governing.

The objection does not seem to hold if we take into account what was said about Saul. Saul possesses the gift of the spirit to rule, and manifests it in a frenetic dance. These men have received a share in Moses' spirit, the spirit of government, and that spirit is manifested initially, once for all, in ecstatic and orgiastic gestures. The manifestation of the spirit for them was in that.

This significant scene with so much to teach could end here, because it tells us about a desire to monopolize all the functions, all responsibilities: a man acquires duties and functions and then complains that he cannot cope with them all. Instead, it speaks to us of a sensible human view that must learn to delegate rather than monopolize. And God sanctions this delegation of authority, power, qualities, as in the liturgy, with a commandment. Moses is not going to be made equal with the members of this senate. Moses continues to be God's confidant. God addresses all his words to Moses and not to the others. He is the head, but this does not exclude the co-responsibility of those below. And God who has made human beings this way sanctions Moses' delegation of power.

Our attention may be drawn to the quantitive form in the sharing of the spirit, as if the spirit were a quantity, instead of an intensity. As if Moses had a hundred and of those hundred, seventy remained to give a little piece to each elder.

48

This is a vision expressed in primitive and simple terms. In this respect it is useful to remember the case of the prophet Elisha, who asks his master before he dies: "give me a double share of your spirit" (2 Kings 2:9).

It is equivalent to asking: make me the heir to your prophetic mission, because the heir, the eldest son, takes a double share. There is a projection of a measurable economic reality on to the spirit, making it quantifiable (into shares and double shares). What happens in the text of Elisha's succession to Elijah is in some way also present here, and we accept it in this poetic narrative.

5. Unexpected appendix

The account might end here with this teaching about the delegation of spirit and its functions. We suspect that this was the case and there existed a separate account of another both prophetic and missionary calling of two persons, who figure with their names and became illustrious in later tradition. Their names are Eldad and Medad. This episode from a different time is found here as an epilogue perfectly connected with what went before. The link lies precisely in the unexpected and the unexpected is about to give us a very important lesson.

God has given an order to Moses: "Choose seventy already trained and fit persons and celebrate a liturgical ceremony by the tent of meeting in a holy place outside the camp and in that ceremony I will distribute spirit and gifts." Moses obeys the order and suddenly the unexpected occurs.

Now two men remained in the camp, one named Eldad, and the other named Medad, and the spirit rested upon them; they were among those registered but they had not gone out to the tent, and so they prophesied in the camp. And a young man ran and told Moses, "Eldad and Medad are prophesying in the camp." And Joshua the son of Nun, the minister of Moses, one of the chosen men, said, "My lord Moses, forbid them." But Moses said to him, "Are you jealous for my sake? Would that all the Lord's people were prophets, that the Lord would put his spirit upon them!" (vv. 26-29).

The scope of this epilogue is unclear and it is precisely this vagueness which makes us suspect it was originally a separate account. It is an anecdote that the author has joined on in a masterly way so that the appendix becomes part of the substance of the narrative.

We may suppose that Eldad and Medad figured in a large record of authorities, but they were not included in the number of the seventy, which on this hypothesis would become seventy-two. The question remains open. And suddenly the unexpected happens: these two men go into a trance, they fall into ecstasy and begin their dancing with frantic gestures which reveal the presence of the spirit. This happens outside the liturgical service, outside the tent, outside the collegiate form. The spirit that has taken them over has dispensed with the rules laid down. Yes, God has prescribed a liturgical ceremony and he has observed it but he has not "tied himself down" with these rules. The spirit has not been "captured" and can act outside the number seventy and outside the rules.

This is the teaching. Anyone who thinks the spirit can be controlled by human schemes is mistaken. The spirit is freedom and is communicated by the tent and in the camp, to the seventy summoned by name and to the other two who are not in the group. The spirit is free, sovereign, it is above Moses and the word, which only has power if it is accompanied by the spirit.

There is confusion and dismay in the camp. Are there seventy or seventy-two? Do the two dissidents have authority or not? Someone immediately goes to tell Moses so that he can restore order. When young Joshua, Moses' faithful servant, hears about it, he feels jealous of his master's prestige. He thinks Moses should exert his authority and absolutely prohibit these manifestations, so that the spirit remains circumscribed within the group Moses himself has consecrated and summoned.

But Moses replies in a noble and open way, which rises above human quarrels. "Are you jealous for my sake? Would that all the Lord's people were prophets, that the Lord would put his spirit upon them!"

Instead of a rebellious and grumbling people, I should like to have a prophetic people, full of the gift of this spirit that has been given to me and the seventy, as it has also to the two who were outside the programme and acting freely. Moses has understood the essence and value of the spirit, but he cannot resist expressing the wish: How I wish all the people were prophets and received the Lord's spirit!

6. Continuation of the theme

Here the account in the book of Numbers ends. To go further we must turn to a text from a probably post-exilic prophet, which announces something spectacular for the times to come at the end. We call this eschatology and the prophet is Joel:

"And it shall come to pass afterwards that I will pour out my spirit on all flesh; your sons and your daughters shall prophesy, your old men shall dream dreams, and your young men shall see visions. Even upon the menservants and maidservants in those days, I will pour out my spirit" (2:28-29).

What Moses asked for as the fulfilment of a dream is announced by Joel as a future reality, without any distinction of sex or age. Let us imagine that the seventy were old and Eldad and Medad were young. It is not in the text but for Joel there is no distinction. The spirit is given to young and old, men servants and women servants... because there is no distinction of sex, age or social class. The spirit will be given to all. This is Joel's magnificent promise fulfilling Moses' generous dream: How I wish all the people were prophets!

Joel's promise remains hanging in the air until the moment of its fulfilment arrives. Its arrival is related in the Acts of the Apostles (2:14-18). Peter and the Eleven succeed in making themselves understood by the motley crowd who have gathered from all the regions of the world and are speaking in many languages. Disconcerted at hearing the apostles speaking in the mother tongue of each one of them, they ask each other what is happening, but cannot explain it, while others mock saying they are drunk. Peter calls for attention and says:

"Men of Judea and all who dwell in Jerusalem, let this be known to you, and give ear to my words. For these men are

not drunk, as you suppose, since it is only the third hour of the day; but this is what was spoken by the prophet Joel:
'And in the last days it shall be, God declares, that I will pour out my spirit on all flesh, and your sons and your daughters shall prophesy, and your young men shall see visions, and your old men shall dream dreams; yea, and on my menservants and my maidservants in those days I will pour out my spirit; and they shall prophesy'" (Acts 2:14-18).

The day of Pentecost fulfils Joel's prophecy, Moses' dream becomes a reality, because the risen Christ has ascended to heaven to send the Spirit of the Father, his Spirit, upon all who believe in him. That gift of the Spirit is a fundamental gift of baptism, which is given without distinction to all who believe in him.

The chapter from the book of Numbers upon which we have commented serves as a starting point for further meditation on the Old Testament's projection onto the New. In our text the people ask for meat and get it, whereas the elders for their part receive the spirit. Meat fills them but produces indigestion, whereas the spirit fills the elders and spreads beyond them.

St John links these themes of flesh and spirit in chapter 6 of his Gospel. Jesus will give the true manna which is his own flesh. "It was not Moses who gave you the bread from heaven; my Father gives you the true bread from heaven" (v. 32). "Your fathers ate manna in the wilderness and they died. This is the bread which comes down from heaven, that a man may eat of it and not die" (v. 50). "It is the spirit that gives life, the flesh is of no avail" (v. 63). The life-giving Spirit also resides in the word: "Lord, to whom shall we go? You have the words of eternal life" (v. 68).

GREGORY OF NYSSA: SPIRITUAL PROGRESS

The perfection of everything which can be measured by the senses is marked off by certain definite boundaries. Quantity, for example, admits of both continuity and limitation, for every quantitative measure is circumscribed by certain limits proper to itself. The person who looks at a cubit or at the number ten knows that its perfection consists in the fact that it has both a beginning and an end. But in the case of virtue we have learned from the Apostle that its one limit of perfection is the fact that it has no limit. For that divine Apostle, great and lofty in understanding, ever running the course of virtue, never ceased straining towards those things that are still to come. Coming to a stop in the race was not safe for him. Why? Because no Good has a limit in its own nature but is limited by the presence of its opposite, as life is limited by death and light by darkness. And every good thing generally ends with all those things which are perceived to be contrary to the good.

Just as the end of life is the beginning of death, so also stopping in the race of virtue marks the beginning of the race of evil. Thus our statement that grasping perfection with reference to virtue is impossible was not false, for it has been pointed out that what is marked off by boundaries is not virtue. I said that it is also impossible for those who pursue the life of virtue to attain perfection. The meaning of this statement will be explained.

The Divine One is himself the Good (in the primary and proper sense of the word) whose very nature is goodness. This he is and he is so named, and is known by this nature. Since then it has not been demonstrated that there is any limit to virtue except evil, and since the Divine does not admit of an opposite, we hold the divine nature to be unlimited and infinite. Certainly, whoever pursues true virtue participates in nothing other than God, because he is himself absolute virtue. Since, then, those who know what is good by nature desire participation in it, and since this good has no limit, the participant's desire itself necessarily has no stopping place but stretches out with the limitless.

It is therefore undoubtedly impossible to attain perfection, since, as I have said, perfection is not marked off by limits. The one limit of virtue is the absence of limit. How then would one arrive at the sought-for boundary when one can find no boundary?

Although on the whole my argument has shown that what is

sought for is unattainable, one should not disregard the com-
mandment of the Lord which says, Therefore be perfect, just as
your heavenly father is perfect. For in the case of those things
which are good by nature, even if men of understanding were not
able to attain to everything, by attaining even a part they could
yet gain a great deal.

We should show great diligence not to fall away from the
perfection which is attainable but to acquire as much as is
possible: To that extent let us make progress within the realm of
what we seek. For the perfection of human nature consists
perhaps in this very growth in goodness.

It seems good to me to make use of Scripture as a counsellor
in this matter. For the divine voice says somewhere in the
prophecy of Isaiah, Consider Abraham your father, and Sarah
who gave you birth. Scripture gives this admonition to those who
wander outside virtue. Just as at sea those who are carried away
from the direction of the harbour bring themselves back on
course by a clear sign, upon seeing either a beacon light raised
up high or some mountain peak coming into view, in the same
way Scripture by the example of Abraham and Sarah may guide
again to the harbour of the divine will those adrift on the sea of
life with a pilotless mind... So we shall take as our model the life
of Moses, as it is presented to us in Scripture.

Life of Moses 5-11
PG 44:400

COMMENTARY

Gregory with his philosophical mind has taken Moses as a
model for a process, not for his individual actions. In Moses he
admires the development of a life, the progress of virtue or
perfection. Human perfection is paradoxical, because in a sense
it consists in denying itself. For the word *perfect* etymologically
means what is finished, achieved. A person who considered
himself or herself finished, or perfect, would be applying a
quantitive measure from within, not an external and supreme
qualitative measure. In virtue also the human being is finite at
every moment, infinite in possibility. As the measure of our

virtue is to share in God, imitating in our own way the Father's perfection, our only possible perfection is to keep going forward. Thus for the human being, being perfect is always knowing oneself to be imperfect and always wanting to be better.

4

Moses' authority

We are going to consider two chapters from the book of Numbers which deal with the theme of authority. Authority shows itself in a particular way in moments of crisis. For what is authority that cannot cope with a crisis? It comes as no surprise that, in human relationships we call hierarchical (superiors and subjects), crises arrive for various reasons, through the fault of one side or another. Where there is human authority, authority crises are bound to arise and Moses had to endure them.

The question is how the crisis is to be resolved. One position states: authority must be defended at all costs, with no concessions, even though objectively it is in the wrong, as if the formal principle of authority were more important than how it serves. Hence authority goes on to defend itself through repression, exacerbating tensions instead of reconciling. Moses received his authority from God and a crisis arises. How does he react? In moments of triumph he has been acknowledged and acclaimed, as the final verse of Exodus 14 says. After the passage of the Red Sea "the people feared the Lord; and they believed in the Lord and in his servant Moses", and they went forward. But at times of misfortune, hunger or thirst or danger, Moses is blamed and his authority disputed.

Chapters 12 and 16 of the book of Numbers give us two examples of authority crises and so we shall consider them together. The first is a family affair, confined to the trio Moses, Aaron and Miriam, a matter between siblings. The second is a complex matter involving the sacred and profane. In both, what principally concerns us is how Moses reacts.

1. The protest

> Miriam and Aaron spoke against Moses because of the Cushite woman whom he had married, for he had married a Cushite woman; and they said, "Has the Lord indeed spoken only through Moses? Has he not spoken through us also?" (Num 12:1-2).

The Hebrew text here begins in a strange way. There are two subjects, Aaron and Miriam, but the first verb is in the singular for "spoke". As if one of the names had been added later. Secondly the protest arises because of Moses' marriage with a foreigner, but the protest itself is about something else. This Nubian woman is not Zipporah the daughter of Jethro. As polygamy was common at that time, it is not extraordinary that Moses should have taken another wife. However, the protest does not say that Moses has done wrong in taking a foreign wife when he could have taken another one from his own people. What is attacked is the principle of Moses' authority.

Because of this incoherence, some authors think that the beginning of this chapter has been manipulated. The figure of Aaron has been added, as well as the matter of Moses' marriage. They corroborate this hypothesis by pointing out that at the end only Miriam is punished, as if she were the only guilty one. This positing of a later elaboration of an original text is plausible. But for our purposes here we are not going into source or redaction criticism. We are merely preparing to meditate on a story by seeking for coherence in the text we have at present.

So, there may be a logical connection between Moses' marriage to the foreign woman and the protest against his authority. Miriam thinks she has found an abuse of authority in her brother's behaviour and claims the right to demand that he give an account of himself or share his authority. As if she were to say: Moses thinks he has the right to take liberties against the customs of our people; as if the commission he has received from God justified all his decisions, including personal and family ones. He thinks he has exclusive authority and does not have to give an account of himself or ask permission from anyone. So he overreaches himself. But he does not have a monopoly of authority, he shares it with us and must take us into account in his decisions.

When the text is read thus, marrying the Nubian woman may be the decision Moses made which was an abuse in the exercise of his authority. Or it may sound like the pretext used to express accumulated resentments. We can also try a psychological approach. The biblical story-teller does not usually stop to analyse and describe the mental states of his characters. He merely describes their actions. We, the readers, can fill in by imagination. Possibly Miriam is jealous of the other woman who enters the household, in case she might rob her of her influence over her brother. Yet another woman and to crown it all, a foreigner! The peaceful family threesome is in danger.

Is Miriam right when she says the Lord has also spoken to them? What has been the role of Moses' brother and sister up till now? Aaron was Moses' mouth in the negotiations with Pharaoh:

"Aaron your brother, the Levite, I know that he can speak well... Speak to him and put the words in his mouth. I will be your mouth and with his mouth, and will teach you what you shall do. He shall speak for you to the people and he shall be a mouth for you, and you shall be to him as God" (Ex 4:14-16).

In another passage:

The Lord spoke to Moses and Aaron, and gave them a charge to the people of Israel and to Pharaoh king of Egypt to bring the people of Israel out of the land of Egypt" (Ex 6:13).

Miriam's role is liturgical. She leads the choir and the dance of the women celebrating the passage of the Red Sea:

Then Miriam, the prophetess, the sister of Aaron, took a timbrel in her hand; and all the women went out after her with timbrels and dancing. And Miriam sang to them: "Sing to the Lord, for he has triumphed gloriously; the horse and his rider he has thrown into the sea" (Ex 15:20-21).

Is this Miriam in Numbers 12 the sister who watched over the baby in the basket on the river and afterwards spoke to the

59

Egyptian princess? Anyone reading these books with a critical eye will immediately think of the different, autonomous traditions with no original relation between them. Anyone reading the account with an eye only for the story will think that up till now we have only been told about one sister of Moses', and unquestioningly identify the two. Or rather, the present account invites us to imagine a Miriam who is older than Moses, who took care of him in infancy, is linked to his triumph and has some ascendancy over him. Strangely this Miriam does not appear to be married and attending to domestic duties under her husband's power (compare Proverbs 31). As a "prophetess" she plays an important role (like Deborah in Judges 4-5).

The threesome has another interesting aspect. In a male-dominated society, the dominant role played by the woman stands out all the more. Both sexes share in the action. Concepts of machismo and feminism are too modern to be projected onto the biblical account. The interesting thing is that God's word is addressed to women just as much as to men. Does this justify the protest of the brother and sister?

2. Judgment and sentence

A simple phrase describes Moses' reaction: "Now the man Moses was very meek, more than all the men that were on the face of the earth." God's immediate intervention leaves no room for further explanations. With God's personal intervention, the question is resolved in a simple way, perhaps too simply, because immediately we go up to the supreme court. In his eagerness for a theological resolution, the narrator compresses the stages and does not exploit the possible story.

God's intervention takes the form of a stylized legal trial. The parties have to appear at the official place of the divine presence, which in the desert is the tent of meeting or appointment. Usually God gives Moses an appointment to communicate his instructions to him. This time all three are appointed to appear. The Lord comes down, as usual, in an upright cloud, "the pillar of cloud", which is the indicator of his veiled presence:

The Lord came down in a pillar of cloud, and stood at the door of the tent, and called Aaron and Miriam; and they both came forward (Num 12:5).

Before this, we have been told "the Lord heard it". Normally the judge must investigate and sift the facts. God sees and hears everything: His is "a jealous ear that overhears everything, not even a murmur of complaint escapes it" (Wis 1:10). Without delay he can pass on to the summing up and sentence.

The crime consisted in disputing Moses' specific authority; the summing up states Moses' privileged status in words that place him in an exceptional position within the prophetic tradition:

"Hear my words: If there is a prophet among you, I the Lord make myself known to him in a vision, I speak with him in a dream. Not so with my servant Moses; he is entrusted with all my house. With him I speak mouth to mouth, clearly, and not in dark speech; and he beholds the form of the Lord. Why then were you not afraid to speak against my servant Moses?" (Num 12:6-8).

We can paraphrase this: I have ministers and servants in my palace or household, whom I trust and to whom I entrust various tasks. But among all of them there is one who stands out for his fidelity and whom I have trusted completely. To the rest I communicate my desires by signs which have to be interpreted or divined: visions, mysterious dreams (here we may recall Jeremiah, Ezekiel and Daniel). On the other hand my prime minister has access and audience with me. He sees my form, he hears me directly, he does not have to guess. If Moses exercises supreme authority, it is because I have entrusted him with it, at first when I gave him his mission in general, and afterwards in the instructions I give him from time to time. He has not taken the authority upon himself, and he has not invented the mission. Now you too hear my words, which are words of accusation. You have had the arrogance to dispute his authority and claim to be equal with him.

In the biblical manner the sentence is contained in the expression "the anger of the Lord was kindled against them".

This anger is not an irrational or uncontrolled passion. It is the judge's just indignation at injustice. Anger against the unjust is love of justice. When the judge feels it and accepts it, it is as a sentence of condemnation. As his sentence is effective it is carried out without fail.

The next scene shows us it being carried out. "When the cloud removed from over the tent, behold, Miriam was covered with a virulent skin disease, as white as snow. Aaron turned towards Miriam, and behold, she was covered with a virulent skin disease." The serious disease which we call vitiligo or leucodermia is the punishment and the penalty. Leviticus describes it with its symptoms in chapter 13. While the disease lasts, Miriam cannot live in the community, she has to live apart and in quarantine. Everyone thinks of her as wounded by God through her own fault, a public punishment.

The reader will wonder why Aaron was not punished too. Apart from the critical explanation we have already noted, we must seek a reason that is coherent within the account as it stands. Perhaps it may be because Aaron, as high priest, has to carry out liturgical functions which are indispensable to the community. Be that as it may, Aaron acts immediately in a function which is very much in accord with his role, and intercedes. Now he does not speak in protest or challenge, but with the humility of a guilty person recognizing his guilt. We should note that he speaks in the first person plural, associating himself with Miriam:

> And Aaron said to Moses, "Oh, my lord, do not punish us because we have done foolishly and have sinned. Let her not be as one dead of whom the flesh is half consumed when he comes out of his mother's womb" (Num 13:11-12).

Like a miscarried child who is not developed enough to go on living by itself; or with its flesh half destroyed by a mortal disease. Although Aaron does not suffer the same punishment he confesses their common sin.

Why does Aaron address Moses and not God directly? Perhaps he feels unworthy to pray to God, even though his office is to intercede. Even though he is physically unharmed and not excluded spiritually from the community, he is far from God and now needs his brother to mediate. He knows his brother's miracle-working power and hopes for a miracle. In fact one of the signs Moses received at the moment of his calling was the infecting and curing of his hand.

The Lord said to Moses, "Put your hand into your bosom." And he put his hand into his bosom; and when he took it out, his hand was diseased, as white as snow. Then God said: "Put your hand back into your bosom." So he put his hand back into his bosom and when he took it out, behold, it was restored like the rest of his flesh (Ex 4:6-7).

What Moses experienced in his own body, he can experience with his sister, who is a blood relation. But besides the physical cure, Aaron asks for an act of reconciliation: let not Moses' concern for his authority be stronger than brotherly love.

If Aaron is directly asking his brother for a miracle, perhaps he is asking him to abuse his power. If God pronounced and carried out the sentence, can Moses interfere and annul it? Wouldn't it be an abuse of the power he has received against the one who gave it to him? But what Moses can do is forgive his brother and sister, and become reconciled with them, and under these conditions he can intercede for them.

And Moses cried to the Lord, "Heal her, O God, I beseech thee" (Num 12:13).

The Lord wounds and heals.(Deut 32:39; Is 19:22; Hos 6:1).

Moses is the faithful and most trusted servant, he deals personally with God. He accepts the reconciliation with his brother and sister and sanctions it: the punishment will only last a week. During this week the whole Israelite camp remains stationary. In silence and without moving they take part in Miriam's penance:

So Miriam was shut up outside the camp seven days; and the people did not set out on the march till Miriam was brought in again (Num 12:15).

The authority crisis has been satisfactorily resolved. Not by repression, not by a purely formal appeal to authority, not by exacerbating the quarrel, but by conviction and reconciliation. God has truly intervened. Which leads to a theological interpretation of the facts and assigning them exemplary value. In a sacred judgment the guilty have been convicted, that is, in a trial. They have confessed their guilt and have asked for forgiveness. Brother and sister began in complicity; their reconciliation with Moses restores harmony between the three. She who was shut out of the community as contagious comes back into it. When the camp sets out on the march the whole community is reconciled. The next stop will be in the oasis of Paran.

3. Sacred authority

Chapter 16 of the book of Numbers is difficult to unravel. A source critic could go to town on this chapter. But even without such an academic analysis, we realize at first sight or hearing that it is a medley of semi-coherent data. Or at least we are aware of the difficulty of following the thread of the narrative. Our task is to meditate on a classic authority crisis, but in order to do so we must first establish a few distinctions.

We see that there are two different rebel groups, with different motives, and they get different punishments. On the one hand there is Korah, who captains a band of Levites and protests against the authority of the priests. The clergy is established in hierarchical form: the Levites or simple clergy form the base; above them are the priests with prerogatives and privileges; and at the top there is the high priest, Aaron. The Levites led by Korah want to abolish the distinctions, and place themselves on a level with the priests.

On the other hand there are Dathan and Abiram, who are not part of the previous group, because Moses has to call them and address them. They are laity, because they belong to the tribe of Reuben (the eldest of the twelve patriarchs). They protest against Moses' authority. Or rather they protest against the way Moses exercises his authority. He has not fulfilled his initial promises, he is failing in his enterprise, he is discrediting his authority, he does not have the right to demand obedience.

At the end the group of Levites with Korah are punished by fire in the ceremony of the censers. The censers were like frying pans: a long rigid handle controlled and supported a metal recipient containing the red hot coals upon which the incense was thrown. The two hundred and fifty Levites came together with the priests holding their censers. The Lord will accept or reject the aromatic offering and thus he will make known whom he has chosen. We can call this an ordeal or judgment of God. When the ceremony takes place "fire came forth from the Lord and consumed the two hundred and fifty men offering the incense".

Dathan and Abiram, who have led a rebellion against Moses' civil authority, die with their families in an earthquake.

And as he finished speaking all these words, the ground under them split asunder; and the earth opened its mouth and swallowed them up, with their households (Num 16:31-32).

With the above distinction the text remains reasonably clear. But another obstacle remains. The first protest of all in the chapter is about something else. It appears to want to abolish the distinction between sacred and profane because the whole people is consecrated.

"You have gone too far! For all the congregation are holy, every one of them, and the Lord is among them; why then do you exalt yourselves above the assembly of the Lord?" (Num 16:3).

God's presence in the camp sanctifies all its members equally and the distinctions are not legitimate. There is no above and below, but equality before the Lord. In Exodus 19:6 God promises that the whole people will be holy, consecrated to the Lord; but there too he adds that they shall be "governed by priests".

Even though holiness is shared out among all through the Lord's presence, there can be degrees in the sharing. This is what the layout of the camp, as described in some chapters of Numbers, is trying to represent in spatial terms. In the centre is the ark of the Lord's presence. Around it there is a first quadrilateral: on the main side are the priests, and the Levites on the other three. Outside this quadrilateral, in squares getting further and further from the centre, are the rest of the people. When services are held the people must stay at a certain distance, the Levites come up to one line and the priests go over it. Within the last enclosure only the high priest can enter, once a year. These spatial dispositions are to symbolize the degrees of sacredness.

The first protest we read about in the chapter sounds like the voice of those who want to abolish the whole hierarchical system, in favour of a sort of egalitarian anarchy. Even though they do not say so, we may recall that hierarchical distinctions did not exist at the time of the patriarchs, who officiated at sacrifices, offerings and blessings. The author who gave the final touches to the present chapter was more concerned to bring data and aspects together than to organize them simply and clearly. (Meditation can move more freely than simple reading. Reading proceeds straight forward whereas meditation can stop and move about in both directions.)

4. The Levites' rebellion

The Levites claim full priestly power for themselves, they do not want there to be degrees in the service of the sanctuary. Let us hear what Moses replies to them, adding comments by way of paraphrase.

"Hear now, you sons of Levi: is it too small a thing for you that the God of Israel has separated you from the congregation of Isaac, to bring you near to himself, to do service in the tabernacle of the Lord, and to stand before the congregation to minister to them...?" (Num 16:9).

"Congregation" is the liturgical name of the community, which is the primary fact. Because they descend from a common ancestor, Jacob = Israel, they all belong equally to it. God, who chose Isaac and not Ismael, Jacob and not Esau, now chooses one tribe from among the twelve. Levites are members of the tribe of Levi. By choosing them he brings them near himself. Drawing

66

near to God is not a human initiative but a divine action, being chosen by his sovereign will. "Blessed is he whom thou dost choose and bring near to dwell in thy courts!" (Ps 65:5). While the rest of the people do military and civil service, the Levites serve the temple cult and "minister to the congregation". Their tasks in the temple are on behalf of the congregation. Their closeness to God is not a privilege for anchorites but a service to the community. "Is that too small a thing for you?"

Moses continues:

> "He has brought you near him, and all your brethren the sons of Levi with you. And would you seek the priesthood also? Therefore it is against the Lord that you and all your company have gathered together; what is Aaron that you murmur against him?" (Num 16:10-11).

Instead of being thankful for what they have received, they protest because they have not received more. Just as Cain could not bear Abel being preferred. Serving God and serving the congregation is their privilege. But they do not do it in a spirit of service but with covetousness and ambition. They are not content with the gift they have received and envy those who have received more or a different gift. Their protest reveals their inner vice, which will make them unworthy even of the gift they have already received. And what is more, although their protest is directed immediately against the head of the hierarchical institution, it goes further up, against God. Because it was not Aaron who chose himself. If God is the creator of the priesthood, the protest is against God, and that is very serious. Those called to serve the Lord are rebelling against him. Can it still be said that they are in his service?

They received a sacred gift and they have turned it against the Lord. So a sacred fire will turn against them and consume them.

> And fire came forth from the Lord, and consumed the two hundred and fifty men offering the incense (Num 16:35).

We can go on reflecting. Moses did not just appeal to his formal authority, demanding obedience: "I order and command.

Aaron has the authority and it is for you to obey and keep quiet". Moses tries to make them understand the mistake they are making and their danger. If ambition enters the servants of God's cult, the whole system will become corrupted and fall into disrepute. Because ambition is a leprosy: like the skin disease which ravaged Miriam's skin. The contagion can consume the structure of the congregation. Korah began it and the two hundred and fifty Levites followed... Where will it end? Those who have not managed humbly to look after the gift they have been given will have it taken away from them. Fire is consecrated by God, not by magic rites. Instead of accepting their fire God turns it against them. Fire will consume those who are already consumed by ambition. Because ambition consumes, it enters the heart and eats it up with ever growing desires that are never satisfied.

Rebellion and ambition, which is more serious? Rebellion can be the reaction of the oppressed or the impatience of the discontented. Ambition corrodes those who are in authority. But "Moses was the meekest of men."

5. Dathan and Abiram's rebellion

Dathan and Abiram rebel against Moses' civil authority. Maybe it is not exact to speak of civil authority, when we consider its divine origin. All Moses' power comes from God and in this sense it is sacred. But when we look at his activity, we can distinguish it from the cultic functions of Aaron, the priests and the Levites. It is possible that Dathan and Abiram led a rebel group, even though the text does not explain the situation. The narrator wants to arrive as soon as possible at the point of maximum tension, in which we see what is at stake. "Moses sent to call Dathan and Abiram the sons of Eliab." This shows us that they did not belong to Korah's group; they are not already there. Moses has the authority to summon the rebels. He does not pronounce sentence immediately or send out a repressive force. He wants to listen to them.

And they said:

"We will not come up. Is it a small thing that you have brought us up out of a land flowing with milk and honey, to kill us in the wilderness, that you must also make yourself a prince over us?" (Num 16:12-13).

The name "land flowing with milk and honey" is the classic formula to describe the promised land. God used it in his first appearance to Moses (Ex 3:8) and it is repeated as a refrain. But the rebels take the name and apply it to Egypt. Egypt, the land of repression and slavery, genocide and forced labour. Such a misrepresentation of the facts is almost blasphemy. Or we could see it as an expression of discontent and nostalgia perversely transfiguring the past. For Egypt was not and never could be a "promised land".

You have brought us out "to kill us in the wilderness". From our sedentary and peaceful life you have flung us into these long marches without direction, without decent living conditions. "You have not brought us into a land flowing with milk and honey, nor given us an inheritance of fields and vineyards." And to crown everything you claim to be our leader. Nothing supports your authority. If you had any, you have lost it. You made magnificent promises and have not fulfilled any of them. We followed you because we were deluded and you have tricked us. Your authority is becoming fatal, it brings death. We do not recognise it any longer.

However, in chapters 13 and 14 of this book we are told about the opportunity they had to enter the promised land and the rebellion of those who refused to go in.

And all the people of Israel murmured against Moses and Aaron... all the congregation said to stone them with stones (Num 14:2, 10).

In the light of these recent events (recent in the narrative composition), the present accusation is seriously unjust: "you have not brought us to a land flowing with milk and honey".

They continue: "Will you put out the eyes of these men? We will not come up." In the literal sense, the curse of blindness (see Prov 30:17). In the metaphorical sense, you want to blind them so that they do not see what is happening, what you are doing. Refusing to come up is denying Moses' authority.

In order to understand Moses' reaction we have to understand that the rebellion is the culmination of a whole series. Moses says to God, "Do not respect their offering. I have not taken one ass from them, and I have not harmed one of them." It is typical of Moses to begin by addressing God; it comes naturally to him. He begins by protesting his innocence to God. Not that he is just and faultless but that the accusations hurled at him are false. In their relations with God human beings are never entirely just. In their relations with others they may be innocent victims. Moses protests: I have not taken advantage of my commission for personal gain or that of my family. I could have asked for a reward for my extraordinary labour but I have not done so. I have not profited even by a single donkey. I have not harmed anyone in the exercise of my authority. I take you, God, for witness. You do not accept offerings from evil-minded and false people.

Then Moses "rose and went to Dathan and Abiram" and in the presence of the people he called on God's justice. Moses does not renounce his authority and cannot do so, because he has been commissioned by God and he can only return it to God. It would be cowardice to give in to complaints and false accusations. He has received authority from God to carry out a giant enterprise. Abdicating, giving up, would be to abandon the task halfway. This would mean condemning the people of Israel to die in the desert. Only God or death will force him to withdraw. There had been a moment (Numbers 11) in which Moses called upon death to free him of his burden and God did not accept his retirement. A day will come when God will require it but that time has not yet come.

Thus God's judgment arrives. The community has to draw away and not take anything from the guilty so as not to become their accomplices. The rebellion must be contained and the innocent not die. "The ground under them split asunder; and the earth opened its mouth and swallowed them up with their households." By eliminating the rebels God wants the march to continue under the leadership of his faithful servant. Moses has authority over the enterprise.

As we finish meditating on this tragic episode, another fire and earthquake come to mind. "I came to cast fire upon the earth; and would that it were already kindled!" (Lk 12:49). This text has been read in different ways. The first, which is the most consistent with the immediate context, refers it to a judgment of separation and purification. The coming of the Messiah is not a trivial or neutral happening. It is a force that consumes the evil and wicked, that kindles the good. Another reading, which is more spiritual and less restricted, refers it to the love that Jesus brings and communicates. Profane and mystical poets like to speak of the fire of love.

> And behold, the curtain of the temple was torn in two, from top to bottom; and the earth shook, and the rocks were split; and the tombs also were opened, and many bodies of the saints who had fallen asleep were raised (Mt 27:51-2).

Christ's death causes an earthquake in the cause of life. The kingdom of death trembles and gives up the dead it had held prisoner.

On the theme of consecration we were thinking about at the beginning of the chapter, we may quote the beginning of the letter to the Ephesians:

> Blessed be the God and Father of our Lord Jesus Christ, who has blessed us in Christ with every spiritual blessing in the heavenly places, even as he chose us in him before the foundation of the world, that we should be holy and blameless before him. He destined us in love... (Eph 1:4-5).

God chooses and consecrates the Christian people as a whole. He consecrates them through his presence in the glorious humanity of Jesus, the Messiah. Love of God and love between humans are the effects of this consecration. If brotherly love reigns authority will not be exercised through ambition or greed, but in a spirit of service, and it will be accepted with affection, not ill grace. And when crises arise, which are inevitable in the human family, they will be peacefully resolved.

GREGORY OF NYSSA: MOSES' BATTLES

> *As long as man is quite weak from ill treatment by wicked tyranny he does not ward off the enemy by himself, because he*

71

*is not able. Someone else fights on behalf of the weak, battering
the enemy with one blow after another. After he is set free from
the bondage of his oppressors, is sweetened by the wood, is
refreshed from his toil at the resting place among the palms,
comes to know the mystery of the rock, and partakes of heavenly
food, then he no longer wards off the enemy by another's hand.
Now, since he has already outgrown the stature of a child and
has laid hold of the vigour of youth, he fights with his opponents
by himself, using as a general no longer Moses the servant of
God, but God himself, whose servant Moses became. For the
Law which from the beginning was given in types and shadows
of things to come remains unfit for battle in the real conflicts. But
the fulfiller of the Law and successor of Moses serves as general;
he was announced beforehand by the name which he shared with
that earlier general.*

*Life of Moses 148;
PG 44:372*

COMMENTARY

Gregory sees in the people of Israel's battle an example of the
Christian's spiritual battle according to the teaching of Ephesians
6:12:

> For we are not contending against flesh and blood, but against
> the principalities, against the powers, against the world rulers
> of this present darkness, against the spiritual hosts of wick-
> edness in heavenly places.

In his final paragraph Gregory alludes to Joshua, Moses'
historical successor. His name is the same as Jesus', his function
prefigures that of the real "successor" to Moses, who is Jesus, the
Messiah. Now it is he who leads our spiritual battle.

As a shadow lacks substance and receives its being from the
solid object that projects it, so the old law is a shadow of the
future, that is, of the Messiah who fulfils it in himself and
simplifies it, and of the Spirit who gives the strength to fulfil it
completely.

5

Moses' prayer

A meditation on Moses' prayer sounds like "prayer squared", because it is praying about another prayer, about another person's way of praying. We might even think that this meditation should not take very long because there is not much to it. Moses' mission is to bring the Israelites out of Egypt and this brings to mind primarily a man of action. In classical terms we might think his life had a lot of the active and little of the contemplative and that a chapter on his contemplation would be bound to be secondary.

Nevertheless something we notice from a first reading is the profusion of texts showing us Moses in the act of addressing himself to God. In this chapter we are not going to discuss the themes of Moses' death, which are to some extent a dialogue with God. We shall also leave out the whole dialogue connected with his calling, which shows us God's entry into the story. We are going to concentrate on very particular moments when Moses talks to God and God, in some way, replies. The first thing that strikes us is how intensely and frequently Moses prays.

We have already noted that Moses is a man of action and this leads him to act towards Pharaoh and organize the leadership of the people. His task, his specific vocation is not to contemplate.

This first difficulty is answered in the Pentateuch accounts where Moses is presented as a man of prayer, although not a man given to long prayers. The books of Exodus and Deuteronomy speak repeatedly of the forty days passed in the mountain, which suggests a long prayer. In these long spaces of time, which nowadays we might call *key times,* Moses lives a life of contemplation, personal dealings with God. The biblical text says nothing in particular, merely stating the fact that he withdrew to the mountain and stayed there for forty days. We know that forty is a round number. But it is highly significant to know that this man of action, called to an epic task, which is clearly an active one, of leading the people out of Egypt, should devote forty days to intimate dealings with God, free from disturbance and the worrying noise of his people. Is this a narrative fiction? Perhaps, but it still indicates the biblical idea that the liberator is first and foremost a man of prayer. Given the number of Moses' prayers, we shall try and put them in order, dividing the material into three asymmetrical and unequal groups.

We shall call the first group *intercession*. Under this we shall place the times when Moses prays for various people apart from himself. The second group will contain prayers of *personal petition*. Of course everything is personal, but here the petition is not for others, but for personal affairs. Finally a third section, the shortest and the most exalted, will study the figure of Moses as *contemplator*, which brings us back to the paradox of Moses the active man who is also a man of prayer.

Moses could think: if I am God's man, I have God's promise and that will do for me. If I am to carry out orders for which God has promised me his assistance I do not need to resort to him. And as a guarantee I hold in my hands a staff capable of performing miracles. He might think he is perfectly well equipped with promises and powers, which release him from the necessity to keep turning to the one who has sent him. But it is not so. In spite of all these guarantees – mission, promise, assistance, staff – Moses constantly turns to God when he runs into a problem or difficulty. At these moments he lifts up his heart, stretches out his hands and prays. This is an important lesson.

Without going into Deuteronomy and leaving aside the texts we have alluded to earlier to which we shall pay special attention later on, we find ten major moments of intercession and then no less than six special pleadings. This statistical fact leads us to the conclusion that Moses the liberator is, above all, a man of prayer.

After this introduction we can now proceed to the first group, prayers of intercession.

1. Intercession for others

To intercede is to ask something for someone else. It comes from the Latin *inter-cedere*. It means coming or standing between two people. Intercession indicates mediation: one person asks a second person on behalf of a third. Moses acts in this triangular way, linking the people and God.

We have spoken earlier of major and minor intercession. We begin with these in ascending scale and we find a first group actually for Pharaoh. The language is repetitive, with variations, and incomprehensible if we do not first imagine Pharaoh's mentality and possible carelessness on the part of the narrator. We have to try to do this first.

Pharaoh is not an atheist or agnostic or a monotheist. He is however a profoundly religious man, with a varied repertory of Egyptian divinities whom he worships. Every people has its divinities, with the providential and protective duty to watch over it. The Egyptian divinities watch over and protect Egypt. Pharaoh as the people's representative has to mediate, offer sacrifices, deal with the priests of these gods. But this totalitarian monarch does not have the God of the Israelites in his pantheon, considering him to be the god of a different community, without any relation or involvement with himself. Pharaoh does not deny his existence. What he does deny is that Yahweh has anything to say to Egypt, for the simple reason that he is a god of another region or people. He respects him as a foreign god but he, the totalitarian and imperial monarch of Egypt, prohibits this foreign god from interfering in the affairs of Egypt. Such is Pharaoh's mentality. The reader has the biblical text and we skip part of the story to the time of the second plague, when the frogs have begun to multiply in an unheard of manner. They jump from the Nile and are infesting all the fields, houses, palaces... They are unbearable and making life impossible.

> Then Pharaoh called Moses and Aaron, and said [sometimes the text speaks of Moses in the singular and sometimes in the plural of both], "Entreat the Lord to take away the frogs from me and from my people; and I will let the people go to sacrifice to the Lord." Moses said to Pharaoh, "Be pleased to command me when I am to entreat for you..." Pharaoh replied, "Tomorrow." Moses said, "Be it as you say, that you may know that there is no one like the Lord our God... And Moses cried to the Lord concerning the frogs, as he had agreed with Pharaoh... and the Lord did according to the word of Moses" (Ex 8:8-13).

We linger over this text, which will reappear later with slight variations. In it Pharaoh appears as someone who knows the name of Moses' foreign God, to whom he attributes the plague of frogs, which his magicians have not been able to stop. The magicians repelled the first plague but they have been powerless against this one. So an intervention by a foreign divinity is required. That is why Pharaoh begs: "Pray the Lord to take away the frogs from my people, because it is he who has sent them; then I will let you go."

Moses asks him for a time and date – we do not know why – and Pharaoh replies: tomorrow. Perhaps he thinks the time is not right and that a particular time is needed to make the prayer work. Moses accepts, giving an explanation: it is not for Pharaoh, through fear or servility, but so that Pharaoh may understand and recognise there is no other god like Yahweh. He does not deny that there are other gods; what he says is that none can compare with Yahweh. Moses cried to the Lord (the verb interceded is not used) and the Lord did according to Moses' word. "Word" has a specific meaning according to who utters it. If God utters it, it becomes a command and the human carries out the command. If a human says it and does accordingly, then it fulfils a promise. In other words: the human obeys God's command, and God carries out the human's petition. This is the suggestive correlation offered to us by the Hebrew formula. Of course: humans cannot give orders to God; what they can do is ask but the effect is the same. They ask and God does what is asked, in the same way as God commands and humans carry out the command.

Now we can review the text at the beginning of Exodus 8. At the end of this same chapter we are told about the plague of flies or gadflies which infest the country. They are unbearable and making life impossible. Pharaoh calls Moses again and asks him: intercede on my behalf. Moses agrees, on condition Pharaoh does not refuse to let his people go. As soon as he has left Pharaoh's presence he intercedes with the Lord and the Lord does according to Moses' word.

The schema is very similar but we should point out certain variations.

Pharaoh asks "Intercede for me", without any explicit allusion to the Lord, the God of Moses. It is equivalent to our expression "pray for me". Moses promises to do so in exchange for freedom. And once he has left Pharaoh's presence he prays to the Lord. In this variant the verb used is always intercede or pray for, but it has an identical result. God did according to the word of Moses, according to the literal Hebrew translation.

In chapter 9 we get the seventh plague. Something happened which never happens in Egypt, a spectacular hail storm, with lightning, thunder and cloudbursts. Because the phenomenon is so unusual and so dangerous to the crops, Pharaoh is frightened and confesses his guilt with the famous formula. "I and my people are in the wrong; the Lord is in the right." In this quarrel there is one who is in the right and others in the wrong. Yahweh your god is in the right; we are in the wrong. And with the recognition of guilt comes his request for prayer to his rival:

"Entreat the Lord... and I will let you go" (v.28).

New elements appear in the prayer rite constituting an interesting ritual curiosity. Moses raises his hands spread at an angle with palms open towards the sky, where God dwells. It is a fine gesture of supplication, like someone holding out an open palm asking for alms. Both hands are held out, separate and open: this is what God sees looking down from above. Moses performed this prayer ritual and the storm ceased. The concession given to Moses' prayer is not explained by relating the petition to the concession: God did what Moses asked. The concession is indicated implicitly: the storm ceased. It is Moses' third intercession in the seventh plague.

In chapter 10 verses 12-20 we read about the plague of locusts and this is the occasion for the fourth intercession.

Then Pharaoh called Moses and Aaron in haste, and said, "I have sinned against the Lord your God, and against you. Now therefore forgive my sin, I pray you, only this once, and entreat the Lord your God only to remove this death from me." So Moses went out from Pharaoh, and entreated the Lord. And the Lord turned a very strong west wind, which lifted the locusts and drove them into the Red Sea.

Of all the formulas this is the one that gives us the clearest idea of Pharaoh's religious position. He begins by recognizing his sin and asking for intercession with the God of Moses.

Yahweh is not his god, but, as he prays to his own god in the affairs of his country, Moses and Aaron must also pray to Yahweh, because it is clear that it is he who has acted in the case of the locusts. And thanks to Moses' prayer the Lord changed the direction of the wind.

It is worth analysing the nuances in this prayer, which cannot be considered as a treatise on the subject, even though there are elements in it upon which to elaborate a theology of prayer. It is interesting how it is told, in the language of common usage and with the repetitions. If Moses is disposed to pray this is not as a purely humanitarian gesture on Pharaoh's behalf: the aim is above all to seek the honour and glory of the Lord. "So that you may know there is no other like the Lord our God;" so that you recognise that the Lord is also sovereign lord of your country. The prayer is regarded from the point of view of and in terms of Yahweh's prestige and glory, whose greatness Pharaoh must recognise. It is a way of praying above all in order that human beings may recognise God's greatness and sanctify his name, without this therefore excluding a human element which takes second place.

We have reviewed a first group of intercessions on behalf of foreigners, strangers, including the great oppressor Pharaoh. And this is where we can best appreciate the human dimension of Moses' prayer. Because he did not pray God to strike his enemy. What Moses asks God is to withdraw the plagues and leave the oppressors in peace, establishing a fundamental distinction between oppression and oppressors, between sin and sinners, and placing God's own glory highest of all.

2. Minor intercessions for the community

In the series of Moses' intercessions we pass from prayer for his enemies to prayer for some members of his community or for the community as a whole. The biblical texts give us an order we want to follow, skipping over the greater intercessions for now to look at the lesser ones. The first one is in the book of Numbers chapter 11 verses 1-3. There is a collective protest which is followed by the punishment of God's anger, which begins to consume the people like fire. The people cry to Moses, he prays to the Lord and the fire stops.

The account is succinct: the people know that Moses enjoys the Lord's favour and turn to God by means of him as intercessor. We know this principle but it is useful to see it confirmed in biblical texts.

In chapter 12 of the book of Numbers we come across a strange protest. The two malcontents are Aaron and Miriam, Moses' brother and sister, who accuse him of being arrogant, and claiming to exert a single absolute authority and making a cult of his own personality. The Lord does not recognise the validity of these accusations and firmly takes Moses' side. Aaron also directly addresses Moses, instead of God, with a plea for forgiveness: please do not hold this sin against us, let not Miriam remain in this state like death. He is speaking of what has happened to her, her hands whitened and paralysed. "Moses cried to the Lord, please heal her." And God accepted Moses' plea and merely imposed on the guilty one seven days' confinement outside the camp. This is another of the moments in which Moses who is accused by his brother and sister, becomes reconciled and intercedes for them.

It is an interesting aspect of intercession: praying for those who have injured him and accuse him in the delicate matter of power abuse. He is reconciled as a brother and intercedes as a mediator with God. Previous reconciliation is a condition of any proper prayer and an indispensable requisite for God to accept the gift laid before the altar (Mt 5:24). Job behaves in the same way when he is accused by his friends; he himself intercedes for them, reconciling them with God (Job 42:8-10).

From here we pass to chapter 16, a complex chapter. In order to make a commentary on it we would need to unravel the threads of two different traditions (see the previous chapter "Moses' authority"). But for the moment we are only interested in knowing that it is about a serious rebellion, with particular ringleaders, who rebel against Moses' authority. The case is particularly grave, because it breaks the unity of a large total plan. In this case Moses intercedes on behalf of the community and, curiously, against the mutinous ringleaders. The rebels are called Korah, Dathan and Abiram. When the devastating punishment begins and they see that God's threat is about to come on the people, Moses and Aaron fall down with their faces to the ground in a position of prayer. It is not the same gesture as arms raised and palms open to the sky, as in the case of Pharaoh. They fall with their faces to the ground in humility and pray: "God of the spirits of all the living, one alone has sinned, are you going to be angry with them all?" The intercession distinguishes between innocent and guilty. In fact the rebel is a group, but it is possible to speak of one alone because this corresponds to one of the traditions. And it separates the rebels from the community. If God is to punish, let the punishment fall on the small group of guilty men who have drawn in other innocent and weak people, but not on the whole community. Moses does not want the affair to be interpreted as general complicity and he does not want the punishment to be indiscriminate. This is the context in which Moses' petition should be set, although it sounds strange and appears negative: "Moses was very angry, and said to the Lord, 'Do not respect their offering. I have not taken one ass from them and I have not harmed one of them" (v. 15). This means: I have nothing to thank them for and I have not abused my position. So, take no notice of them, do not accept their unjust offerings. These men have rebelled, provoking God's anger, and it is necessary to ask that that anger should fall on them and not be extended to the whole community.

This is double intercession, with the two faces of guilt and innocence.

In chapter 16 we find another intercession with some new perspectives. This is another case of protest in which the whole community is involved. The fire of divine punishment begins burning the camp, taking some victims. The nature of their action is not made specific, and it can even be read as a repetition of the case mentioned before. Moses reacts by addressing Aaron:

> And Moses said to Aaron, "Take your censer, and put fire therein from off the altar, and lay incense on it, and carry it quickly to the congregation and make atonement for them; for wrath has gone forth from the Lord, the plague has begun. So Aaron took it as Moses said, and he stood between the dead and the living" (16:46-48).

This is a new example of ritual intercession. Here we do not have words which have an effect on things. Here it is a person who goes to confront the fire of God's anger, irreconcilable with sin. Fire tamed in the service of the cult in the censer will burn up the grains of aromatic resin made by a tree and turn it into perfume rising up to God. This aroma is the sacrifice of the earth, and it signifies the acknowledgment of a fault to God and the desire for purification. This rite has to be practised by Aaron, the priest who performed the priestly functions, in order to celebrate Moses' liturgy of intercession. They know that this liturgical act is going to have an effect, and in order to make the symbolism more vivid Aaron stands between the dead and the living as an impassable barrier. The consuming fire, which has already begun to destroy and is trying to spread, meets the impassable barrier of this column of aromatic smoke and it stops in front of it. The fury of the punishment also stops, pacified by Aaron's ritual intercession. From here we jump to chapter 20, to read the story of the water. The people are dying of thirst and protest to Moses, demanding water to drink. God is going to punish this protest, but Moses and Aaron draw apart from the community, go to the door of the tent of meeting and fall face downwards on the ground.

A highly significant detail occurs here. The intercessors withdraw from the community, but this withdrawal does not mean spiritually distancing themselves from the people, but coming nearer to them. In their intimate appointment with God in the tent of meeting they feel closer to the community and intercede effectively for them. The physical distancing is necessary for the spiritual coming closer. God comes down to the appointment and Moses and Aaron fall face downwards on the ground, in a gesture of humble vassalage. Then the glory of the Lord appeared in luminous splendour without shape or form. God spoke to Moses and ordered him to go to the rock and command it to gush forth water to drink. And we have the episode of the Waters of Meribah.

In chapter 21 there is a plague of poisonous serpents in the desert. The people come to Moses and confess their sins:

"We have sinned for we have spoken against the Lord and against you; pray to the Lord that he take away the serpents from us." So Moses prayed for the people. And the Lord said to Moses, "Make a fiery serpent, and set it on a pole" (vv. 7-8).

The people begin by confessing their sin. The offence is principally against God, but also against Moses: we have spoken against the Lord and you. Their repentance is the only argument the people can invoke in seeking Moses' intercession: you must pray for us. He allows himself to be satisfied with this confession and returns to his function of intercessor. He cannot be cruel, he cannot seek revenge; he has to accept generously and forgive: and Moses prays to God on behalf of the people.

This is the formula for intercession on behalf of a third party. Moses prayed on behalf of the people and God heard him and gave him an order. We have studied six cases of Moses' intercession. We have called them "minor" and in them we have been seeing in small but significant detail the way to engage in prayer of intercession.

3. Major intercessions

Now we can pass on to the major incidents of intercession corresponding to chapters 32 and 14 of Exodus and Numbers respectively. The latter is a duplicate of the former and so it will suffice to expound the great intercession in chapter 32 of Exodus, divided into two parts, the first from verses 1 to 14, the second from 30 to 35.

When the people saw that Moses delayed to come down from the mountain, the people gathered themselves together to Aaron, and said to him, "Up, make us gods who shall go before us; as for this Moses, the man who brought us up out of the land of Egypt, we do not know what has become of him." And Aaron said to them, "Take off the rings of gold which are in the ears of your wives, your sons, and your daughters, and bring them to me." So all the people took off the rings of gold which were in their ears, and brought them to Aaron. And he received the gold at their hand, and fashioned it with a graving tool, and made a molten calf; and they said, "These are your gods, O Israel, who brought you up out of the land of Egypt!" When Aaron saw this, he built an altar before it; and Aaron made proclamation and said, "Tomorrow shall be a feast to the Lord." And they rose up early on the morrow, and offered burnt offerings and brought peace offerings; and the people sat down to eat and drink and rose up to play.

And the Lord said to Moses, "Go down; for your people, whom you brought up out of the land of Egypt have corrupted themselves; they have turned aside quickly out of the way which I commanded them; they have made for themselves a molten calf, and have worshipped it and sacrificed to it, and said, "These are your gods, O Israel, who brought you up out of the land of Egypt." And the Lord said to Moses, "I have seen this people, and behold, it is a stiff-necked people; now therefore let me alone, that my wrath may burn hot against them and I may consume them; but of you I will make a great nation."

But Moses besought the Lord his God and said, "O Lord, why does thy wrath burn hot against thy people, whom thou hast brought forth out of the land of Egypt with great power and with a mighty hand? Why should the Egyptians say, 'With evil intent did he bring them forth, to slay them in the mountains, and to consume them from the face of the earth'? Turn from thy fierce wrath, and repent of this evil against thy people. Remember Abraham, Isaac and Israel, thy servants, to whom thou didst swear by thine own self, and didst say to them, 'I will multiply your descendants as the stars of heaven, and all this land that I have promised I will give to your descendants, and they shall inherit it for ever.'" And the Lord repented of the evil which he thought to do to his people (32:1-14).

On the morrow Moses said to the people, "You have sinned a great sin. And now I will go up to the Lord; perhaps I can make atonement for your sin." So Moses returned to the Lord and said, "Alas, this people have sinned a great sin; they have made for themselves gods of gold. But now, if thou wilt forgive their sin – and if not, blot me, I pray thee, out of thy book which thou hast written." But the Lord said to Moses, "Whoever sinned against me, him will I blot out of my book. But now go, lead the people to the place of which I have spoken to you; behold my angel shall go before you. Nevertheless in the day when I visit, I will visit their sin upon them."

And the Lord sent a plague upon the people, because they made the calf which Aaron made (32:30-35).

Moses did not go to the tent of meeting, a few paces distant from the camp. This time he went up through the surrounding hills further into the mountain, far from the people and alone with the Lord. What had been envisaged as a brief visit is becoming unduly prolonged, and the people begin to suspect that the Lord may have carried him off with him. And if Moses does not return they foresee a serious and tragic situation. Far from Egypt and deprived of their leader what can they do camped in the middle of the desert? They need to seek a substitute, another effective guide. Moses' delay and the urgency of the situation drive the people to apply in massive numbers to Aaron, demanding "Make us a god to go before us, because this Moses who brought us out of Egypt we do not know where he is or what has happened to him." Come on, make us a god!

But can a god be made? Can a human artefact become a god? It is God who makes human beings, not human beings who make God. Nevertheless human beings have frequently tried to create God. In primitive cultures this was done in a more material and crude way: a piece of cut wood, a carved stone... have served to suggest a divine presence. In higher cultures gods are created in the mind: human beings make their own gods in their hearts and minds and then confuse their own ideas of God with God himself. An idea of God is not God. God is always beyond, above all ideas and formulations, because he is always totally "Other". Formulations are a way of trying to come closer to God but never to possess or manipulate him. It is not for human beings to make gods but to recognise that God made us and we are his (Ps 95). Make us a god! the people beg. As if Aaron through being of priestly stock had a superhuman and super-divine power to make gods. Of course it is not a question of making a god but an image of God, but what do they want this image for? They want it go in front of them and this suggests a reflection. It is like a workman who wheels his barrow of bricks along a twisty, narrow, muddy path, or across a pit by means of some wobbly planks, to where he unloads them. The man faithfully follows the barrow: wherever the wheel goes he goes behind it, to the right or left... and it occurs to us to ask which is leading which? The man goes behind pushing the unmotorized wheel by two handles: wherever the wheel goes he goes too but which is leading which?

The people of Israel ask for a god to go in front of them. They want a manageable god, to which they can put wheels and handles, a stone, metal or wooden image they can take wherever they want. The human mind creates concept-wheelbarrows, by which it can comfortably transport its god and follow it. Which is leading which? We have constantly to revise our image of God to see if we are following him or figments of our imagination adapted to suit ourselves.

The people of Israel now do not know what to do with this God who brought them out of Egypt; they do not know what has happened to him; or perhaps it was not him but Moses; or perhaps both. But now both have gone away and they need to make another god to go before them.

> [Aaron] received the gold at their hand, and fashioned it with a graving tool, and made a molten calf; and they said, "These are your gods, O Israel, who brought you up out of Egypt!" (32:4).

According to the text it seems that it is an image made of molten gold. But we could also imagine – more probably – that it is a large wooden image, which was then gold-plated, because if it was solid gold and natural size it would be very difficult to handle. But this is a secondary detail. The important thing is that Aaron gave in to the people's request and made the calf they had asked for.

In many ancient religions the bull is one of the symbols of powerful and fertile divinity; the bull is not God but it can symbolize this fertile power of the divinity. Aaron gives the idol this form, which is completely forbidden in Israel, because the people have recently subscribed to a formal covenant, one of whose clauses prohibits them from making images of the divinity.

> "You shall not make yourself a graven image, or any likeness of anything that is in heaven above, or that is in the earth beneath, or that is in the water under the earth" (Ex 20:4).

One clause of the covenant prohibits the making of images even of Yahweh. Why? Because of the danger that through the images the people claim to possess, dominate or manipulate the divinity; a manageable divinity ceases to be a divinity: it is purely the work of human hands.

This is hinting implicitly at a theology which will later become clear and explicit: no images must be made of God because the moment God becomes manageable and under human control, he automatically ceases to be God.

We are in the Old Testament but we cannot ignore what Aaron says: this strong, gold-plated calf that you see before you is your God, who brought you out of Egypt. Aaron does not deny this God's historical category; he does not translate the God of the Exodus to the Olympus of mythology, he does not make him a cosmic God. This God is still the God of the Exodus, and the crime consists in having tried to shape him in disposable and manageable form. In order to demonstrate that it really is the same God, Aaron built an altar and proclaimed: tomorrow there will be a feast of the Lord.

In fact next day a great liturgical festival is celebrated, a sort of day of obligation or great solemnity.

We can defend the people by invoking their ignorance and lack of insight. The people do not know theology or understand the stipulations of the covenant. What the people want is to have a God present who seems to be absent, God of the covenant, expressly Yahweh. The bull is a form of Yahweh's presence. They do not deny the fact of their exodus from Egypt; they recognise this great benefit and act with good will. Aaron is the guilty one. His priestly training should have sharpened his awareness and refined his critical judgment about different ways of worship. But the people are innocent.

This line of excuse is not acceptable. However much goodwill they may have had, it is not sufficient to justify their worship taking this form. Because although on one level their intention is good, on another (deeper) level it is totally wrong. With good intent they want to celebrate the feast of a god represented in the shape of a bull, which they will carry through the desert. But however well meaning they may be they are indulging in a radically depraved form of religious behaviour: this is not God and cannot be God. Their good intentions do not prevent their falsification of the divinity. The God who brought them out of Egypt is above and below, before and after, he is sovereign and not at their disposal, whereas the god they have made to go before them is a god at their disposal, tame and manageable and therefore cannot be God. Although it may appear to be God, it is an idol, and religion based on faith in this god is depraved and false. The narrator is well aware of this. From the festive scene that is taking place in the valley with singing and dancing, party and banquet, he goes up the mountain and in a bold stroke he shows us the true God, true religion, represented by a genuine man of prayer: Moses.

Here begins the great dialogue, one of the peak moments in Moses' life and of prayer in the whole of the Old Testament:

> And the Lord said to Moses, "Go down; for your people, whom you brought up out of the land of Egypt have corrupted themselves" (v. 7).

We must pay attention to all the nuances, especially the play of subjects and attribution of complements: "*Your* people whom *you* brought out of Egypt." Who brought them out and to whom does this people belong? God says to Moses, but Moses replies with the same words, as if excusing himself, justifying himself, saying: I did not more than obey your orders, it is *you* who brought the people out.

God takes the initiative, can take it at any moment. At that moment a human being might hear an insistent inner voice, which is identifiable without any possibility of doubt as God's voice. Moses' calling is one of those moments when God takes the initiative; but the present case is not like this. Moses has withdrawn from the people and is living in the mountain in retreat for high contemplation, and there at a certain moment God's word comes. The man has to arrange appropriate circumstances on his own account. Then God presents himself and speaks: Come on, go down from the mountain... It is an accusation as if he were to say: "Moses, you are responsible for this people, you brought them out of Egypt. I am telling you what is happening so that you may take appropriate steps." Their great crime is that a human artefact is officially and solemnly declared to be the God of Israel.

It is not apostasy from Yahweh; it is the identification of the sovereign, transcendent and holy God with an image made by human hands. Now it is for God to pronounce sentence, because the people have broken one of the solemn clauses of the covenant. They cannot seek the excuse of ignorance or forgetfulness because the covenant is recent, it was made almost yesterday.

The Lord unburdens himself to Moses: I see that this is a stubborn people, stiff-necked as a young bull that shakes off the yoke and becomes threatening. So God says: "Let me alone: the fire of my anger is going to blaze against them and consume them and I will raise a great people from just you." It is the threat of punishment and the hope of a promise. It is like saying: I cannot fulfil my historic plan with this rebellious and insubordinate people. Let me wipe them out, Moses, and I will begin again with another people born of you.

How is it that God asks Moses' permission? Who is putting God at man's disposal, Moses or God himself?

We have seen that Moses lives in an intense atmosphere of prayer and in this state he is capable of picking up subtleties of tone or listening to whispers. It is a delicate game: Let me, that is to say, don't let me; you can let me or not, but I hope you will not let me: I lay the decision in your hands. It is like a street quarrel between two men in which the one who feels offended starts shouting as he fluctuates between his outrage at his impugned honour and his striving not to hurt: Stop me or I'll kill him!, which means: he deserves it but I don't want to do it.

Thus God expresses his feelings concerning this people who are no good for his historic project. So is everything over? No; from you I will bring forth a great people.

Let us listen carefully to this sentence; it is the same word as God addressed to Abraham. It is the great patriarchal promise of fertility. When the world has become corrupted and God decides to begin a new era with Abraham, the latter is still just one man. But God promises: from you I will bring forth a great people and with this people I will begin to carry out my project of salvation.

Now the people have failed. God wants to eliminate this people who are no good and begin again with Moses, who will be the new Abraham. Because this people – your people – is no longer good for anything, but I can distinguish perfectly between you and your people and I shall not consume you with them. In the case of Korah, Dathan and Abiram, Moses intercedes for them: it is one who has sinned, so do not get angry with all. Here it is the other way round: all have sinned except for one, and God promises to save him and make him a great patriarch.

Moses also has experience of the people being stubborn and difficult to manage. Won't the idea of beginning a peaceful patriarchal life attract him? He could look forward to a glorious future with a new and docile people and a new covenant. Moses has caught the subtle tone of this "let me" and he pacifies the Lord saying: "O Lord, why does thy wrath burn hot against thy people, whom thou hast brought forth out of the land of Egypt with great power and with a mighty hand?"

And he carries on arguing: "Why should the Egyptians say, 'With evil intent did he bring them forth to slay them in the mountains, and to consume them from the face of the earth'?" That is, take care of your good name, Lord. What you did to your people in bringing them out of Egypt was a public act, plain for the nations to see. The most powerful empire on earth was present at it. They have been told that it was the work of Yahweh, our God. The Egyptians know it and when they realize that this same people liberated from Egypt have perished in the desert they will laugh at you, saying this is an impotent God who brought them out and then let them die, a vengeful God who deceived them by bringing them out to finish them off in the desert. So what will become of your fame and your good name then, Lord? You presented as credentials to your people your concern for their state of slavery, your affection and compassion for the weak and oppressed. But now you are going to behave like a vengeful God in whom no one can trust. Have you thought this out carefully? Lord, if not for the people, do it for your name, your glory. Curb the fire of your anger, repent of your threat against your people. Your anger is legitimate, because it is indignation against sin, and the holiness of your being can never make a pact with evil. All this I know, but I will not let you. Restrain your anger and withdraw your threat against your people.

And he continues with a third final argument, whose force must be read between the lines, with sharp eyes and ears: Remember your servants, Abraham, Isaac and Israel to whom you swore by yourself, saying: "I will multiply your descendants as the stars of heaven, and all this land that I have promised I will give to your descendants and they shall inherit it for ever".

Moses goes back to before the exodus from Egypt: to the promise to multiply the people and possess the land. The people is this one, the one that has come out of Egypt; what they still lack is possession of the land. If you annihilate them now, the people will have come to an end, you will have broken the promise to the line of Abraham, Isaac, Jacob and his twelve sons. It is true that God can destroy the people all except for Moses and thus the line will not be broken, because Moses is descended from Abraham, and the people born from Moses will continue to be descended from Abraham, only having to suffer the delay of two centuries, which is nothing to God. If Moses draws apart from the people and accepts God's offer the promise will not be broken. It will only be deferred. But if Moses sides with the people and prays: if you destroy them all, destroy me too with them, then the promise will be broken that God cannot break.

God could say: I am going to fulfil it in you. But Moses does not accept this. In this way he ties God's hands by interceding for his people and identifying with them, not with their sin, but with their punishment.

"And the Lord repented of the evil which he thought to do to his people." Moses intercedes not from above, not from outside, not from far away, but from among them. This is his great intercession.

> On the morrow Moses said to the people, "You have sinned a great sin. And now I will go up to the Lord; perhaps I can make atonement for your sin." So Moses returned to the Lord and said, "Alas, this people have sinned a great sin; they have made for themselves gods of gold. But now, if thou wilt forgive their sin – and if not, blot me, I pray thee, out of thy book" (vv. 30-32).

Either all or none. I do not want to be treated as priviliged; I share the fate of all. If you are going to eliminate them all, then also blot out my name. This is a noble example of intercession, not from a distance but in solidarity.

The figure of Moses is not exhausted in this supreme moment of his life. Moses is acting as the figure and type of another great intercessor: Jesus, who became one with us, our brother in all things except sin, who shares our fate including death. And thus as one of us, a brother among brothers and sisters, he can intercede with the Father and obtain forgiveness for all humanity. Moses' intercession is the high point of his life, which enlarges his shadow till it reaches the height of Calvary, from where we hear another intercession: Father, forgive them for they know not what they do.

We can complete the picture with another great moment of intercession, which is a replica, repetition or variant of the former. We find this in chapter 14 of the book of Numbers and it is inserted into the episode of the rebellion of the scouts. The people of Israel have arrived from the south to the frontiers of the promised land. Now they only need to do battle and take possession of it. But Moses decides to send on ahead a group of scouts to spy out the land in its positive and negative aspects. The scouts return with ambivalent information, ambiguous: the land is excellent, but its inhabitants are fearsome. The land is magnificent and we should like to possess it but we cannot do anything against its inhabitants. At this information panic breaks out in the community. Only two of the scouts, Caleb and Joshua, remain faithful to Moses. The others rebel and decide to stone Moses and Aaron, and once they have got rid of them return to Egypt, undoing all that has been done.

Here the sin is not making an idol or manufacturing an image of Yahweh to manipulate at will. Here they want to abandon the Lord altogether. They are going to undo history, go back along the road they have come by to where life is better, in Egypt, the land of oppression. This denial of God and his salvation is a very serious crime, which also threatens the lives of Moses and Aaron. What do they do? They turn to God and pray. This intercession picks up some of the themes from chapter 32 and develops them, introducing variations and stressing certain aspects:

And the Lord said to Moses, "How long will this people despise me? And how long will they not believe in me, in spite of all the signs which I have wrought among them? I will strike them with the pestilence and disinherit them, and I will make of you a nation greater and mightier than they" (Num 14:11-12).

91

Here we have the theme of punishment which will put an end to the people. But one member will be saved who will be the founder of a new patriarchal dynasty.

But Moses said to the Lord, "Then the Egyptians will hear of it, for thou didst bring up this people in thy might from among them, and they will tell the inhabitants of this land" (v. 13).

Now it is not only the Egyptians, but the Egyptians will carry the news and Yahweh, the god of the Israelites, will be universally discredited:

"They have heard that thou, O Lord, art in the midst of this people; for thou, O Lord, art seen face to face, and thy cloud stands over them and thou goest before them, in a pillar of cloud by day and in a pillar of fire by night" (v. 14).

That is, they know about the leaving of Egypt and the series of miracles you have been performing up to the present, so to fail now is much more serious than at the beginning. They will think this God lacks the strength to go on supporting his people; he is a magnificent but limited God, since he was able to begin but unable to carry it through to the end.

"Now if thou dost kill this people as one man, then the nations who have heard thy fame will say, 'Because the Lord was not able to bring this people into the land which he swore to give them, therefore he has slain them in the wilderness.' And now, I pray thee, let the power of the Lord be great as thou hast promised, saying, 'The Lord is slow to anger, and abounding in steadfast love, forgiving iniquity and transgression, but he will by no means clear the guilty, visiting the iniquity of fathers upon children, upon the third and upon the fourth generation.' Pardon the iniquity of this people, I pray thee, according to the greatness of thy steadfast love, and according as thou hast forgiven this people from Egypt even until now" (vv. 15-19).

Moses' intercession invokes the commitments made by God and this God's real nature which is to be merciful and

92

compassionate. God could interrupt the enterprise and still remain unharmed; what he cannot do is go against his nature. Moses does not urge the people's merits, which do not exist, but the consequences of God's own merciful and compassionate nature. This is a new element which did not appear so clearly in the previous intercessions. The figure of Moses stands out nobly as the figure of the great intercessor.

4. Personal petitions

Now we shall give our attention to five special moments in which Moses addresses a personal petition to the Lord. In the previous intercessions he was praying for someone else, Pharaoh, the people, his brother and sister... In these he prays for himself, although always in relation to the mission he has been given. These five examples refer indirectly to the people, but directly and immediately they have as their object personal affairs of Moses, not excluding the aspect of the public person in him.

The number five is interesting in itself. We have listed twelve intercessions, ten minor and two major. But here we have just five personal prayers, three minor and two other greater ones. The work of meditating will be much simpler in this part, but again we find evidence of the spontaneity with which Moses addresses God whenever problems arise in the fulfilment of his mission.

Let us skip back and be present at the moment in which Moses is about to present himself to Pharaoh. These are the first skirmishes before the terrifying plagues. Moses has to ask the omnipotent Pharaoh to end the oppression and free his people, but the powerful king replies viciously, turning the screw tighter and imposing new burdens on the people. At that moment of general discouragement among the people, Moses turns to God and says:

O Lord, why hast thou done evil to this people? Why didst thou ever send me? For since I came to Pharaoh to speak in thy name, he has done evil to this people, and thou hast not delivered this people at all."

But the Lord said to Moses, "Now you shall see what I will do to Pharaoh" (Ex 5:22-23; 6-1).

This is a prayer in the form of a reproach, which clearly reveals a certain intimacy between Moses and God. This tone of reproach is not a challenge, and we should hear the tone of familiar confidence between two people who love each other and reproach each other freely in formulas such as: why...? How is it possible...? in which there is more tenderness than protest. The content does not consist simply in saying "Amen". Moses opens up trustingly in prayer and unburdens himself freely to God.

A second moment takes place just after the passage of the Red Sea, when they are faced for the first time with the problem of lack of water. The thirsty people come to a spring, but the water is salty. Protests arise and Moses turns to God, who shows him a plant. Moses throws it into the water and the water becomes drinkable (Ex 15:25).

The passage is succinct but it serves as evidence: when in difficulty Moses cries to the Lord and is heard.

The same water problem arises on another occasion, this time in chapter 17:4:

Moses cried to the Lord, "What shall I do with this people? They are almost ready to stone me." And the Lord said to Moses, "Pass on before the people."

Moses addresses God but the reproach falls on the community. Indirectly it is also directed at God, because he has not taken care on his own account of this rebellious people. It was God who put him over them, and therefore it is for God to solve the problem. It is a model attitude on Moses' part, addressed to God in a tone of humble and familiar reproach.

The fourth moment is more substantial. It is a continuation of the great intercession in chapter 32. The problem is: Will the Lord go on accompanying us until the promised land or is our crime so great that we are not going to be able to count on him? Moses' prayer is intense and reiterated, and we have just one bit of it in chapter 33. This chapter must be read and meditated on with care, so that we do not lose a single detail: it is all important.

Moses said to the Lord, "See thou sayest to me, 'Bring up this people'; but thou hast not let me know whom thou wilt send with me. Yet thou hast said, 'I know you by name, and you have also found favour in my sight.' Now therefore I pray thee, if I have found favour in thy sight show me now thy ways that I may know thee and find favour in thy sight. Consider too that this nation is thy people."

The passage tells of a sort of quarrel between Moses and God. We have already indicated that Moses' prayer does not consist in saying "Amen" to everything, but in open dealing with God, without deception, because trying to deceive God would be deceiving oneself. Moses modestly says what he feels: You have entrusted me with an enterprise, but I am alone for the task and you do not tell me who can help me, in spite of my being your friend and confidant.

It is a fine way to pray to God because it is arguing with him in his own words, without twisting them, as Job did at one point and Satan too in the temptations in the desert. Twisting God's words is not appealing to what God has said. In negotiations between friends they appeal to a word that has been given: you yourself said this, you promised... And this manner of reasoning with God in his own words is a good way of praying, because it denotes knowledge of what he has said. Arrival at this point means you have come a long way along the road of prayer.

God promises him: very well, I shall go in person. And Moses grasps hold of this promise and reinforces it: all right, because if it is not this way do not order us to move; it must be made known somehow that I enjoy your favour and that this people is your people. God has appeared on Sinai, and there the great experience of the covenant has taken place; also the great tragedy of the first sin and the first forgiveness. But everything is not over, there has been a very important pause, a fundamental one, along the road from Egypt to the promised land. There is still a long way to go and this difficult people must be able to rely on a companion for their journey. Moses, Aaron and the elders are not enough. God himself must accompany them, and thus it will be noticed that this people is different from others: God is their travelling companion along the path of life.

And God answers Moses: I will also grant this request of

yours because you enjoy my favour and I treat you personally. By his prayer Moses has at last dragged out God's own admission: you enjoy my favour and I treat you personally.

Let us now jump to chapter 11 of the book of Numbers, the most intimate and significant, bold and instructive.

The people have received the miraculous food from God, the manna, which punctually comes down from heaven during the night, so that they can have their daily bread and continue their journey. They even get double rations on Fridays so that they can eat and rest on the Sabbath. But the people get fed up and bored with this diet: always the same single dish! We have spent a long time in the desert and we are missing the food in Egypt. We want different food. Another rebellion!

Moses heard the people weeping throughout their families, every man at the door of his tent; and the anger of the Lord blazed hotly, and Moses was displeased. Moses said to the Lord, "Why hast thou dealt ill with thy servant? And why have I not found favour in thy sight, that thou dost lay the burden of all this people upon me? Did I conceive all this people? Did I bring them forth, that thou shouldst say to me, 'Carry them in your bosom, as a nurse carries the sucking child, to the land which thou didst swear to give their fathers? Where am I to get meat to give to all this people? For they weep before me and say, 'Give us meat, that we may eat.' I am not able to carry all this people alone, the burden is too heavy for me. If thou wilt deal thus with me, kill me at once, if I find favour in thy sight, that I may not see my wretchedness" (Num 11:10-15).

Everything is marvellous in this prayer. It seems important to add a commentary without taking anything away from the original enchantment of the familiarity and intimacy with God, the skill in making God understand what he is suffering, the loving complaint and the cautious boldness: "Why do you ill-treat your servant?" If a master ill-treats the only servant he has, who is the loser, the master or the slave? I am the Lord's servant not on my own account, but because he has taken me into his service and I have managed to be faithful. Now this master pays for my fidelity by ill-treating me. He does not beat me, because

I enjoy the privilege of his favour, but he throws a burden on my shoulders that is beyond my strength, that burden of a whole rebellious and difficult people. Lord, you throw this burden on me without measuring my strength and you flatten me. Where will you find another servant as faithful as I am? Free me from the burden of this people; I am not their mother. Why have I got to be burdened with them and carry them in my arms as if I were their nurse?

Like an underlying base we can just hear in this prayer a second voice: Who is the mother of this people? It is God and it is up to him to take care of them and feed them day by day. Let God show his motherly yearning and tenderness. I am only God's officer. I love this people, but I cannot cope with them. They cry like babies and when I give them something to eat they demand something else and they are never quiet or satisfied with anything. If I have to serve you in these conditions, crushed by the weight of my responsibility, repaid by protests, and if I truly enjoy your favour, it is better to die. Lord give me death!

God answers him with a double promise: for the meat problem he miraculously sends flocks of quails; for the problem of the burden of the people he orders Moses to share the work with a senate of seventy elders.

This was the theme of another meditation.

5. Contemplation

The third part of Moses' prayer is the highest and the least explicit. Having arrived at this level of intimacy and contemplation a person experiences much but there is very little that can be said about it. Nevertheless we can pick out various passages from the books of Exodus and Numbers which enable us to get a certain idea of Moses' contemplation. We are going to go backwards, beginning with an explicit testimony in a text we find in the book of Numbers (12:1-8).

There is a rebellion. Rebellion is nothing new, but this time it has the strange particular that the rebels are Moses' own brother and sister: Miriam and Aaron. In this episode we are interested in what is going to be said about Moses' role. (See the previous chapter "Moses' authority".)

And the Lord came down in a pillar of cloud and stood at the door of the tent, and called Aaron and Miriam; and they both came forward. And he said, "Hear my words: If there is a prophet among you, I the Lord make myself known to him in a vision, I speak with him in a dream. Not so with my servant Moses; he is entrusted with all my house. With him I speak mouth to mouth, clearly and not in dark speech; and he beholds the form of the Lord. Why then were you not afraid to speak against my servant Moses?" (Num 12:5-8).

When we read these words we are bound to think of Moses as a high prophet. He is not just a messenger, an envoy from God, who hears words and faithfully transmits them; he is a confidant who has easy access to God's presence. He is not an employee, a bureaucrat or an official, not even a minister. He is much more than any of these. God speaks in a vision to prophets and tells them things in dreams through images and figures. Dreams show the figure, the image, the vision, the word that the prophet hears and can identify as God's word. Moses is not like this. Moses, says God, is my servant, my intimate personal friend, the most faithful of all my household, and I can trust him as no one else. Therefore I speak to him mouth to mouth – or we would say face to face – I get on with him as when a friend speaks face to face with another friend and he does not need to interpret enigmas because he sees my form.

The author is trying to suggest an idea to us: here we do not have dreams or images; here we have an immediate closeness in direct dialogue with God, whom Moses does not need to guess at because he speaks face to face with him. God calls him to listen in silence and then he repeats what is said to him.

The text does not give us any particulars. It merely draws aside the veil of the mystery and allows us to gaze in amazement at Moses' relationship with God: mouth to mouth dialogue, direct contemplation of God's form.

The second example comes in chapter 24 of Exodus, where we hear about Moses' going up to contemplate the Lord.

The Lord said to Moses, "Come up to the Lord, you and Aaron, Nadab and Abihu, and seventy of the elders of Israel, and worship afar off. Moses alone shall come near to the

Lord; but the others shall not come near, and the people shall not come up with him" (Ex 24:1-2).

Here we have steps in a hierarchy which perhaps translate liturgical customs. The people remain below in the foothills, on a terrace or plateau, the seventy go up, who are not all the elders, senators or councillors of Israel, but a select group who work together directly with Moses in the carrying out of ordinary business. After the group of priests there is the top figure of Aaron and with him Nadab and Abihu: seventy four people in all.

They all go up the mountain and reach the top. There they stop and prostrate themselves, in a gesture of vassalage. Moses detaches himself from them and draws near to where the Lord is to deal with affairs personally with him. It is like a centre, surrounded by a circle like a barrier and down below the whole community waits: it is one of the data. The other is the permission to see God. Moses, Aaron, Nadab and Abihu and the seventy elders of Israel went up and saw the God of Israel: beneath his feet he had a sort of sapphire pavement, like the sky itself (Ex 24:9-10).

Nothing is described of the figure of the Lord, only the platform on which he rests his feet. As if there were a second firmament according to ancient ideas, like a luminous vault or tent. God is in heaven above the firmament, and when he comes down the mountain has another sky, another vault, which is in some way a replica of the heavenly one and is indicating God's greatness and sovereignty. With a double function it veils and reveals both at once. But God did not lay his hand on the chief men of Israel because he himself had called them. "They beheld God, and ate and drank," that is, they had a banquet.

This account also seems very bare to us. A few people are invited to a very special contemplation of God and something is said about him similar to what we find in chapters 10 and 11 of Ezekiel. We feel there is an effort to say how he was, what he was like. We are not told directly. The author of this fragment gives up any attempt at describing him. He merely speaks of a presence which Moses and the chosen group were able to contemplate but not to pass on to us. The example of Moses can be an invitation to go up and look, contemplate even though these are things impossible to talk about.

A third step would lead us to speak of Moses' periodical meetings with the Lord in the tent of meeting. We shall devote a special meditation to it with the title "Moses and the Glory". Naturally it belongs to "contemplation", but it is so important that it deserves to have a meditation to itself.

Let us now pass to the last fragment, sublime and enigmatic pages charged with religious experience.

Although God communicated with Moses without enigmas, this communication reaches us wrapped in veils of mystery which only allow us to glimpse or guess something. We shall interweave a text with quotations from Exodus 33:18-23 and 34:5-8.

God has told Moses: you enjoy my favour, I deal with you personally. Immediately Moses takes this statement by God to throw out his last and boldest request: "Show me your glory".

And God said: "I will make all my goodness pass before you, and will proclaim before you my name 'The Lord'; and I will be gracious to whom I will be gracious, and will show mercy on whom I will show mercy. But," he said, "you cannot see my face; for man shall not see me and live" (33:19-20).

Here we are told what God is going to give and what he is going to refuse. He will let all his wealth and goodness, all his majesty pass by (and Moses can actively contemplate them) for God is supremely good. In the creation story after every work it is repeated: "and God saw that it was good". But "good" also means beautiful: everything that God made at the beginning was good, because the Lord only makes good things. But better than everything and all things together is the supreme goodness himself, and he is going to make this goodness pass before Moses' astonished eyes. Why? "Because I will be gracious to whom I will be gracious, and I will show mercy on whom I will show mercy". It is pure benevolence on God's part: a human being cannot demand or claim anything; it is not a reward for services rendered, everything is pure generosity on God's part. Moses is going to be one of the ones God favours.

The first condition for this gratuitous contemplation is humility. There are no merits or claims. Because God favours whom he wishes to favour, Moses can see his goodness and his majesty

100

passing by; then he will hear his name, "Yahweh," but not pronounced by himself because he is mortal. He will be able to hear how God pronounces his own name but he will not be able to see God directly "because no one can see God's face and live".

But if God's presence means death to human beings, how can we speak of a good God?

God is so good, so great, that a human being cannot contain him. A person might die in a terrible spasm of unbearable pain, and the intensity of the pain be what causes death. Might not an intensity of joy also overflow human capacity and paralyse the heart in an ecstasy of joy? Human beings are to some extent unlimited, they can broaden their capacities, but God will always be too much for them, because God cannot fit in a human mind or heart. If these tried to contain God they would explode and die. If a human being were to see God he would die from the excess of beauty, too much greatness. So the mystics say. In contemplation they have reached a point which enables them to glimpse with a guarantee of certainty what God really is, beyond what they have been able to learn. And because it seems to them that now they touch him, that he is within a hand's reach, but in reality he is on the other side, they want to die, they ask to die to be able to leap over to the other side by death and have the power to grasp him with new eyes. This is the supreme moment of mystical contemplation.

The biblical text hints at something of this. Its best commentators are not the professional exegetes who analyse the signs of the Hebrew text, but those who have been admitted to the high and profound experience of the Lord. Humans cannot see God's face and live; it is too much for creatures; they will see it later, from the other shore.

> And the Lord said, "Behold there is a place by me where you shall stand upon the rock; and while my glory passes by I will put you in a cleft of the rock, and I will cover you with my hand until I have passed by; then I will take away my hand, and you shall see my back; but my face shall not be seen" (33:21-23).

Once again the author is dealing in enigmas, the mysteries of God. The mountain is a privileged observation point with many possibilities, and among others there is a special observatory. There is a cleft, a sort of natural niche in the rock. In this cleft, protected from everything by the rock and only able to look outwards, Moses will be able to see from the top of the mountain the unique vision of God's shining glory passing by. It is too much for a human being. It dazzles, it could blind him to the point of killing him. So God will cover the cleft with the palm of his hand with no gap between the fingers, so that Moses does not die. Thus he will have the sensation as of God's palm becoming translucent with a glow shining through but he will not be able to see God himself. And when the splendour of the glory has passed, God withdraws his hand. What does Moses see then? God's face? No, he sees his back, the form of his going away, God's withdrawal.

What more can be seen? God approaching and going away. At the peak moment of contemplation in this life a man sees God going away, because God is always "beyond". The more we plunge in his ocean, the deeper it gets. The more we see of him, the more we see the limitlessness of the "wholly Other". We never approach the limit, only the limitless. Therefore the further we advance in contemplation, the greater we discover God to be; we experience being brought close to God in order to see him withdrawing. The same thing happens when an astronomer observes a planet; the planet is there, exciting his curiosity, as it speaks to him of a sun in the centre of that system; the astronomer focuses and gazes at the central star and that star focuses him and draws him towards the greater distance of the galaxy. As he peers and scans the horizon of dark space he sees the universe's limits stretch further and further. He sees how these spaces astronomers call infinite prove to be infinite indeed and therefore go on and on.

Thus we see God going further and further off; we do not see God's distance but God going away. Closeness remains on the other side of death.

"The Lord descended in the cloud and stood with him there, and Moses proclaimed the name of the Lord" (34:5). It is curious that in similar texts there is a certain ambiguity as to the person who is speaking.* Our interpretation of the text suggests that at

*In the RSV translation it is the Lord, not Moses, who speaks.

this moment – when the Lord comes down and Moses feels his presence – Moses pronounces Yahweh's name, and when he utters it, the same word echoes back. But perhaps the human echo, the voice bouncing off a slope or sheer rockface, comes back with some mountain harmonies. In the present case it is not Moses' voice that is given back by the rock: it is God himself who utters his own name and titles, which must be listened to thus, because when a human being pronounces God's name his lips diminish it. God's name must be invoked humbly and then we must listen in silence to hear it uttered by God himself and see how it sounds. Who can tell?

The author does not say. He only tells us the words that Moses hears in that ineffable, unique, penetrating and enveloping tone. There is no human language capable of reproducing that tone. Nevertheless, let us listen to God speaking of himself, pronouncing his name and attributes:

The Lord passed before him, and proclaimed, "The Lord, the Lord, a God merciful and gracious, slow to anger, and abounding in steadfast love and faithfulness, keeping steadfast love for thousands, forgiving iniquity and transgression and sin, but who will by no means clear the guilty, visiting the iniquity of the fathers upon the children and the children's children, to the third and fourth generation" (34:6-7).

If the dialectic of evil and human sin reaches even the thousandth generation, so does the influence of God's goodness. St John appears to be echoing these words when he speaks of God's fullness (Jn 1:16). Of this fullness of steadfastness, goodness and faithfulness we have all received, as grace responding to his grace; because no one has ever seen God, not even Moses. Moses could speak of this goodness and faithfulness, but he could not see God. The only begotten Son of the Father is the one who has made him known.

As we read this account of Moses, we should ask for the gift of contemplation, which cannot be gained through our own merits, but can be asked for in humility from the Lord who is faithful and rich in mercy, and we can prepare ourselves for it. As Christians, we listen to the Son's voice, that reveals the Father's face: "he who sees me, sees the Father" (Jn 14:9). It is

Jesus who makes us listen, in words and deeds, to God's fullness: fullness of steadfastness, goodness and faithfulness.

God proclaims his greatness, puts out the palm of his hand and lets his glory pass by; when he withdraws his hand, Moses sees God going away and is left only with the form of his retreat.

ORIGEN:
MOSES' INTERCESSION

The Lord says to Moses: "I will put an end to them and from you and from your house I will bring forth a large nation, much larger than this one." He utters this threat, not to indicate that the divine nature is subject to anger, but in order that Moses' love for his people may be shown and God's goodness to the sinner. It is written that God was irritated and threatened to put an end to the people in order that it might be seen how far human beings can go with God and the confidence they may have because the divine indignation is assuaged by human pleading and human beings can make God change his purpose. The kindness that succeeds the anger shows Moses' confidence in God and how the divine nature does not give way to anger.

The text also contains a mystery that will be fulfilled in the future, that is, that God, rejecting that people will raise another. He says: "I will put an end to them; from you I will bring forth a great nation." This threat is not anger, but prophecy. He will choose another nation, the people of the Gentiles, but not through Moses. Moses excused himself because he knew that the great nation promised would not be named by him but by Jesus Christ and it would not be called the Mosaic people but the Christian people."

PG 12:621

Origen finds two lessons in Moses' intercession. The first, more obvious one, is the power of human pleading addressed to God. In this Moses does not have a monopoly but offers an example to all. The second lesson he calls "mysterious" because it refers to Christ and his Church. Origen's reasoning can be schematized thus: From you I will bring forth a great people – says God. Moses distinguishes: a great people, a universal people, yes; from me, no. Because I am not the Messiah and the universal people will come from him; the Christian people, from Christ.

GREGORY OF NYSSA: MOSES' CONTEMPLATION

How does someone who Scripture says saw God clearly in such divine appearances – face to face as a man speaks with his friend – require that God appear to him, as though he who is always visible had not yet been seen, as though Moses had not yet attained?

The heavenly voice now grants the petitioner's request and does not deny this additional grace. Yet again he leads him to despair in that he affirms that what the petitioner seeks cannot be contained by human life. Still, God says there is a place with himself where there is a rock with a cleft in it into which he commands Moses to enter. Then God placed his hand over the mouth of the hole and called out to Moses as he passed by. When Moses was summoned he came out of the cleft and saw the back of the one who called him.

What then is being signified? Bodies, once they have received the initial thrust downward, are driven downward by themselves with greater speed without any additional help as long as the surface on which they move is steadily sloping and no resistance to their downward thrust is encountered. Similarly, the soul moves in the opposite direction. Once it is released from its earthly attachment, it becomes light and swift for its movement upward, soaring from below up to the heights.

If nothing comes from above to hinder its upward thrust (for the nature of the Good attracts to itself those who look to it), the soul rises ever higher and will always makes its flight yet higher – by its desire of the heavenly things straining ahead for what is still to come, as the Apostle says.

Made to desire and not to abandon the transcendent height by the things already attained, it makes its way upward without ceasing, ever through its prior accomplishments renewing its intensity for the flight. Activity directed toward virtue causes its capacity to grow through exertion; this kind of activity alone does not slacken its intensity by the effort, but increases it.

For this reason we also say that the great Moses, as he was becoming ever greater, at no time stopped in his ascent nor did he set a limit for himself in his upward course. Once having set foot on the ladder which God set up (as Jacob says), he continually climbed to the step above and never ceased to rise higher, because he always found a step higher than the one he had attained.

He shone with glory. And although lifted up through such lofty experiences, he is still unsatisfied in his desire for more. He still thirsts for that with which he constantly filled himself to capacity, and he asks to attain as if he had never partaken, beseeching God to appear to him, not according to his capacity to partake, but according to God's true being.

Life of Moses 219-20; 224-6; 230;
PG 44:399, 400, 403

6

Moses and the glory

Chapters 32-34 of the book of Exodus are a transcendental focus for Moses' life, because they offer a mature vision of the great leader in his personal relations with God. Chapter 32 is the high point of his intercession. As a whole what is described here is the vain wish to see what is invisible, because no one can see God and live. In what follows we shall look at another scene, regularly repeated, which tells about Moses' intimate personal dealings with God, which make him the mediator of the divine presence among the people. We find this passage in chapter 34 verses 29-35.

1. Moses

When Moses came down from Mount Sinai, with the two tables of the testimony in his hand as he came down from the mountain, Moses did not know that the skin of his face shone because he had been talking with God. And when Aaron and all the people of Israel saw Moses, behold the skin of his face shone and they were afraid to come near him. But Moses called to them; and Aaron and all the leaders of the congregation returned to him, and Moses talked with them. And afterwards all the people of Israel came near, and he gave them in commandment all that the Lord had spoken with him in Mount Sinai. And when Moses had finished speaking with them, he put a veil on his face; but whenever Moses went in before the Lord to speak with him, he took the veil off, until he came out; and when he came out, and told the people of Israel what he was commanded, the people of Israel saw the face of Moses, that the skin of Moses' face shone; and Moses would put the veil upon his face again, until he went in to speak with him.

The text appears to speak of a single isolated case. But if we combine this piece with the fragment we read in chapter 33 verses 7-11, and taking into account a phrase we read in passing, we can deduce that this experience is a repeated fact of life for Moses. At the moment when he comes down from the mountain something new begins which is then repeated every time that Moses goes to visit and have personal dealings with the Lord. The fundamental thing here is the glory or splendour. This is the theme of our reflection.

The glory is the manifestation of the God of Israel without form or figure. The Hebrew word *kabod* is related in its root to notions of weight and volume – as in Latin *gravitas*. But the Old Testament texts that speak of the glory of the Lord relate it more to luminousness or splendour. Light is a total presence, single and enveloping but formless. In this sense the Lord's glory is like an enveloping presence, a very intense luminosity, on which human beings cannot fix their eyes without going blind and dying. If seeing the light is living, to stop seeing the light is dying. The light of God's presence is so dazzling that human beings cannot bear it. That is why it is said that human beings cannot see God and live.

God gave Moses an appointment on Sinai to seal the covenant with him and give him the commandments, which are the stipulations of the covenant. Moses had a personal encounter with the *glory* as God's intense presence. The biblical text also speaks of intercession and other details, among which we note the fact of what happened in this personal encounter between Moses and God.

Moses has left the deep valley to go high up, where the air is purer and the light more intense, and there he has been exposed to the Lord's resplendent glory. And the Lord's light has transfigured him without his being aware of it. His face has become radiant, not with its own radiance, but reflected, so as to become a mediating agent of God's presence. The text expresses it in these terms: "his face was shining". Our metaphorical expression is "he became radiant". Its original meaning is that it sends out light rays and this is precisely what we have in the original text referring to Moses, making it clear that the light source is not Moses himself. By a sort of photoelectricity or phosphorescence, through being exposed to God's radiance,

Moses has become radiant himself. And when he comes down from the mountain and reaches the valley again, where the people of Israel are waiting impatiently for him, they can see that Moses has a radiant face. In this luminous radiance they recognise a reflection of God's glory.

This episode can be related with a verse at the beginning of Genesis: God created man in his own image (1:26). But the case of Moses has something special about it. It is not so much an image as a communication, and hence, a resplendent mediation of God's glory. The people's reaction is fear, as if in the presence of God himself. They cannot look at him, or hear his voice, nor that of the thunder which shakes the mountains. They feel a reverential fear of Moses, because he bears a new presence. The people do not dare go near him. But Aaron and the other leaders of the community approach Moses, and he speaks to them not just as any man but as a "radiant one". Everything he says is a resonance of God, in the same way that everything the people see is a splendour or reflection of God.

Later, the people decide to approach Moses cautiously; they are full of reverent fear. To dissipate this fear, to soften his presence and mitigate the radiance, Moses throws a veil over his face. But the people of Israel recognise that behind the veil there is a splendour, which has sprung directly from the divinity.

The radiance and the speaking go together. The radiance is like a necessary halo surrounding the oracle, the mediator. Moses brings both God's word and light. The light convinces the people of Israel that the word comes from on high, and so they receive it as such. The text tells us that Moses communicated God's message first to Aaron and the leaders, and afterwards to the people. Radiance, glory and message go together.

But the narrator gives us to understand in the last paragraph that this first impressive encounter which once took place on Sinai is going to recur periodically. It is as if the Lord did not tell him everything there all at once and he still has many things to say. There is much to be said and many things to consult about. It will be necessary to renew this personal encounter daily or periodically. Now the meeting will not take place on the mountain but in the tent of meeting or appointment, according to the correct translation of the Hebrew *mo'ed*. It is not said that God lives in a tent. But the people do. The people of Israel live in a camp of tents, and among these there is a special one dedicated to the divinity. But the divinity is not there permanently. Just from time to time he comes there to an appointment with Moses. Therefore it is called the Tent of Appointment or Meeting. This meeting is repeated periodically as we are told in the second text, which gives new details:

> Now Moses used to take the tent and pitch it outside the camp, far off from the camp; and he called it the tent of meeting. And every one who sought the Lord would go out to the tent of meeting, which was outside the camp. Whenever Moses went out to the tent, all the people rose up, and every man stood at his tent door, and looked after Moses, until he had gone into the tent. When Moses entered the tent, the pillar of cloud would descend and stand at the door of the tent, and the Lord would speak with Moses. And when all the people saw the pillar of cloud standing at the door of the tent, all the people would rise up and worship, every man at his tent door. Thus the Lord used to speak to Moses, face to face, as a man speaks to his friend. When Moses turned again into the camp, his servant Joshua the son of Nun, a young man, did not depart from the tent (Ex 33:7-11).

What happens in these periodic, almost daily, meetings? The same thing as once happened initially on Mount Sinai: God visits the tent with his formless glory and floods Moses with his splendour. Moses speaks with the Lord, becomes impregnated with his light until his face is transformed and when he comes out of the tent, it is radiant. The people see it, they prostrate themselves reverently and listen to his words, which are the words of God. Because the Lord spoke to Moses face to face as a man speaks to a friend.

This expression is very intense, although it is formulated as a comparison. In human beings the face is in effect a means of communication because through it the soul is glimpsed. More exactly, the soul becomes present in the face with its affections and feelings. The expression "speak face to face" faithfully translates the original Hebrew *panim' el-panim*. Moses spoke with the Lord as a man speaks with a friend, that is, face to face, without veils or distance, feeling a friendly presence in the familiar face.

110

This way of speaking seems to attribute a face [*panim*] to God. We have to take it as metaphorical and understand the expression in a limited sense. Here the face [*panim*] is God's presence. It is not bodily with form or figure but a presence that Moses feels as we feel the presence of a friend when we are speaking face to face. If we must not exaggerate the idea of a figure or image, neither should we minimize the idea of an intimate personal relationship. *Panim* also alludes to the personal and a correct translation could be: God spoke personally with Moses. He does not speak personally to the people of Israel but through a mediator. With Moses he speaks personally, and the result is that Moses comes away from the meeting shining anew and the people are frightened. This is why Moses veils and unveils himself. When Moses goes out to the tent the people of Israel feel a tremble because they know that he is going to meet the Lord. It is a sacred moment. And when Moses comes out of the tent, he throws a veil over his face so as not to dazzle the people who listen to the particular message communicated by God to Moses. These details are repeated at every meeting.

So in these two fragments of the book of Exodus we have a legendary and magnificent vision of Moses, which enables us to glimpse something of what this intimate dealing between him and God means, an encounter which is contemplation and listening, wordless contemplation and silent listening. Here the figure of the great leader becomes gigantic as it is offered to our respectful consideration.

The second fragment mentioned above also speaks of the cloud:

> When Moses entered the tent, the pillar of cloud would descend and stand at the door of the tent, and the Lord would speak to Moses. And when all the people saw the pillar of cloud standing at the door of the tent, all the people would rise up and worship, every man at his tent door (Ex 33:9-10).

What does the cloud refer to or what is the point of it? It is a frequent theme in the Old Testament. The cloud is the veiled presence of the Lord. It is his *elusive* presence, says a commentator. The cloud enables us to see when the sunlight dazzles us. Its edges, its margins are radiant, and the cloud is luminous in its way. It reveals and conceals. Through the cloud we know something of the presence of the sun. Looked at straight the sun would dazzle. But the cloud comes between and gives us a veiled view of it. The Old Testament and especially these accounts use the cloud as a symbol for the presence of God. He comes *veiled* in the cloud. His presence has to be discovered gradually through these veils, until you come to the final revelation without veils, which is what Moses wants but cannot have. This recalls the poem expressing the desire: Uncover your presence!*

Uncovering his presence is taking off the veil. This is the particular detail linked to the theme of the tent of meeting. The cloud stops at the door. It is a witness that the Lord is inside. It is as if the cloud is standing guard. The people of Israel understand, they feel the Lord's presence and they prostrate themselves in worship. Then a second moment comes: when Moses comes out the cloud rises and God goes away. It is the end of the appointment. And Moses comes radiant to speak to the people.

2. Psalm 34

Psalm 34 is going to provide us with the second point of this meditation. A characteristic note of this psalm is that it appears to rehearse what St Ignatius of Loyola later calls *application of the senses*, a form of contemplation which mobilizes or applies some of the senses to the mystery contemplated. Psalm 34 speaks of seeing and hearing God, which is a frequent theme and it also speaks of tasting him – a less frequent idea – savouring the Lord's goodness and tastiness. We shall not attempt to develop this theme, but we do want to note the importance of the theme of glory in relation to contemplation. Our attention is concentrated on a verse of this psalm which links directly with our two texts from Exodus on Moses' glory. The Hebrew text does not use the same word, but it does deal with the same theme and moves in the same imaginative world of the luminous and shining. Psalm 34:5 says, "Look to him, and be radiant" (meaning, look at the Lord).

*The Bride speaking in the *Spiritual Canticle* by John of the Cross.

In this psalm a liturgy leader is addressing a community, probably present in the temple, to invite them to a prayer of praise: Bless the Lord all nations... The invitation to speak is extended to experiencing God. People should not behave as if they knew everything or as if faithfully following a pre-made plan. They come to the temple not only to sing or to ask, but also to contemplate. You have to interrupt the programme and pause to contemplate God. For this another image helps, that of *tasting*, which is mentioned later in verse 8: O taste and see, O taste, savour and appreciate how good and tasty the Lord is. In contemplating the same thing happens as in tasting. You do not swallow a tasty thing at once, but savour it slowly on your palate to appreciate and enjoy its taste. Neither can contemplation be hasty. It cannot consist in a torrent of words which we ourselves say. It is much more a question of silence, opening up passively to God's presence in order to contemplate it. So if you lay yourself open to God's presence in a sort of spiritual nakedness and silence you become radiant. The reflections of the glory of Moses we considered before seem to reach this far. But what was the exclusive privilege of the great man is now offered to the whole community. We could call it a sort of democratization of the experience of the Lord. Now all can be like Moses. In contemplation there is no difference. The Lord is not limited to the tent of meeting but inhabits the temple permanently, in the middle of his people. They have to go to the temple, enter its courts and contemplate a presence. And anyone who really has contemplated it will become radiant like Moses. That unique and solitary historical experience becomes a paradigm. Because this is not a psalm of Moses. The psalm is not telling the unique experience of a privileged person but is an invitation to repeat that great experience again and again. So this psalm which is a prayer is at the same time a lesson: we are to pray but praying is not enough; as well as this we are to contemplate, we are to savour God. And all who have really had the experience of this contemplation of God will be transfigured, illuminated by an inner light that does not come from themselves but from outside them. The shining illuminates their faces and they become radiant. Contemplate him and you will become radiant. It is a text with a message and motto which should be taken to heart and put into practice.

3. St Paul

The third point takes us into the New Testament, in particular, Paul's second letter to the Corinthians. It is an important text. It is a free commentary by Paul on the story of Moses with the shining face and the veil he threw over it. It is not a commentary of modern exegesis. Paul follows the practice of his time and makes a Midrashic commentary in which, from the biblical data, a new reflection is elaborated. The biblical account remains but it is used, even amplified, as a mould or vehicle for a new reality. And here Paul is insisting on the *newness*. The free movement of Paul's thought gives us a clarifying commentary on this difficult text so that we can make it the theme of our meditation. The effort will be repaid by the splendid definition of what a Christian presence can be in modern society, a secularized world. At the end we shall linger on this point. For the moment let us look at the text of 2 Corinthians 3, from which we shall select some phrases which are like a programme or summary of what will be said later. Paul is dealing with the theme of apostolate. Because he is an apostle Paul feels responsible for a very important mission, even more important than that of Moses. These are very strong words. They are said by a true Jew, a man familiar with the Torah for whom Moses and David are the greatest figures in the national history. Verses 4-6 can introduce us to the subject:

> Such is the confidence that we have through Christ toward God. Not that we are sufficient of ourselves to claim anything as coming from us; our sufficiency is from God who has qualified us to be ministers of a new covenant, not in a written code but in the Spirit; for the written code kills, but the Spirit gives life.

In the Greek original, *código* is the letter, a written thing that is opposed to the spirit. Paul is referring to the written record of the old covenant, which can be called the code. It is the letter, there are stipulations. And as Paul is going to speak so highly of his apostolic mission, he feels obliged to make a prior declaration of humility: I do not want to claim anything for myself; everything I am going to say I have received from God. Even personal qualities are a gift of God. So if we can glory in anything, it is not in personal merits but gifts of God.

This is a small introduction so that he does not sin through immodesty. Rather than indulging in vainglory he is defining a new reality in contrast to another. The new reality is that Paul, the apostle of Jesus Christ, is the mediator of a better and more important covenant than the former one. This new covenant is not based on a written record or a code of stipulations; it is linked to the Spirit.

In our modern culture we also require signed and sealed written documents for legal validity. Perhaps word alone is not enough. But there are other commitments between people which are as serious or even more so, even though they do not depend on written documents. This is the contrast Paul introduces before beginning his commentary on the passage about Moses and the glory. So we come on to the study of the two covenants, based respectively on the code-letter and the spirit. Then we shall look at the agents or mediators of these covenants. The agent of the old covenant is Moses, that of the new is Paul in relation to the communities founded by him thanks to the Lord's message. Here he recalls the splendour of Moses, the agent of the old covenant, but introduces an unexpected element. We must begin by quoting 2 Corinthians 3:7-8:

> Now if the dispensation of death, carved in letters on stone, came with such splendour that the Israelites could not look at Moses' face because of its brightness, fading as this was, will not the dispensation of the Spirit be attended with greater splendour?

We find it strange to hear that that covenant and code were agents of death. Does this mean a total condemnation by Paul of the Sinai alliance as an agent of death? The expression is very strong. We need to reflect quietly on these paradoxical expressions of Paul's so as not to mistake him.

The Sinai covenant established a community and linked with God a community among whose members liberty and justice reign. This covenant was articulated in a series of commands. Firstly, the basic stipulations which we call the "ten words", the

"Decalogue", then a broader series of prescriptions. And it is all recorded, not on parchment or papyrus but on tablets of stone so that it remains for ever. It is to be lapidarian. It will be preserved within the Ark of the Covenant, in the alcove of the temple, as one of its most sacred objects. It is the testimony in stone between God and the people, which the people have undertaken to observe. But as well as the stipulations there is a catalogue of promises and threats. If the people keep it, they will have life and prosperity on earth; if they break it, they will lose their land and life. Prosperity and life are now linked to the fulfilment or non-fulfilment of the covenant. The content of these precepts is, of course, good and for the most part permanent, because they reflect radical requirements of human nature. Some of their elements are known in other cultures. But this good content is a law, that is, a series of orders from outside which impose requirements on people without at the same time giving them the strength to fulfil them. Lured by other interests, ensnared by other slaveries to selfishness and sin, people do not keep these rules and thereby fall into crime and pain of death, they do not deserve prosperity and lose the land. The people are guilty of death. Something similar happens to the garden of Eden: if you eat from this tree, you are guilty of death. So, paradoxically, the result is that what was given for the life of the people becomes in fact an agent of death, through the people's fault and because an external law does not at the same time automatically give the strength to keep it. So is there a need for a new law? That one was not sufficient. As long as it is an external legislation engraved with writing on stone, the same thing will happen again. The system must be changed, the text corrected. The new system will be the rule of the Spirit. This is the meaning of the paradoxical phrase that sums up Paul's thinking and which he develops in other passages.

Paul goes on: the old covenant was like that and in spite of its limitations, Moses, its agent – he who communicated it to the people – came radiant. Because he had talked with God and brought word from God which was valuable in itself, Moses came resplendent. "So should not the dispensation of the Spirit be attended with greater splendour?" The apostle (Paul in this case for the Corinth community) is not the agent of an external written text, but of the Spirit of the Messiah who gives himself to the believer through faith. Paul is an agent of the Spirit. Therefore he too shares in Moses' splendour, and more so than Moses.

For if there was splendour in the dispensation of condemnation, the dispensation of righteousness must far exceed it in splendour (v. 9).

It is now clear what is meant by *condemnation; rehabilitation* makes us righteous, not guilty and in a serene relation to God.

Indeed, in this case, what once had splendour has come to have no splendour at all, because of the splendour that surpasses it. For if what faded away came with splendour, what is permanent must have much more splendour (vv. 10-11).

That one and this one, the fading and the permanent. Paul uses a comparison with light to show the difference. A faint light lit at night pierces the darkness and the space round the light is lit up. But if a big fire is lit beside it or the sun comes out, the first light disappears, not because it fails but because it does not show, "for when the sun shines the stars have no light". This is what happens, says Paul, with the old and the new covenant. Compared with the agent of the Spirit, who is the apostle, we have to conclude that the former fades away as if it did not exist (vv. 10-11). And Paul goes on to the consequences for apostolic life which are also for Christian life. For this he takes up the theme of the veil that Moses threw over his face :

Since we have such a hope, we are very bold, not like Moses, who put a veil over his face so that the Israelites might not see the end of the fading splendour (v. 12).

This is clear. The apostle of the Messiah must have his face uncovered, without deception or pretence. He cannot hide or keep anything back, because his message is for all. Unlike Moses his face must be uncovered and open. Moses' veil softened his splendour so that he did not dazzle; but the Israelites did not enter the mystery, which remained veiled from them. Its meaning was not just God's presence there at that moment, but also the annunciation of a presence to come. Here we come to the new element introduced by Paul, who speaks of its *purpose* (*telos*). The original expression can mean end or purpose. Perhaps it is word play. On the one hand the Israelites do not realize that all that is fading, has an end. And they do not understand either that that which fades has as its purpose to announce, amid veils of mystery, the coming of the new covenant. Moses' veil prevents the Israelites penetrating the mystery and they remain outside. "But their minds were hardened. When they read the old covenant that same veil remains unlifted, because only through Christ is it taken away."

Now we have Paul's play on ideas. According to the Exodus text a veil covers Moses' face. Paul develops this to assert that the veil covers the readers' eyes, coming between them and the Old Testament writings. For since Christ's coming the whole of the Old Testament is clothed in a new light. The veil has fallen away and new depth and height and fullness of meaning appear which were veiled before. Christ has taken away the veil and the old becomes new. Origen wrote: "The Old Testament was old but since Christ's transfiguration and glorification it has become gospel." Because with the light it receives from Christ it reveals Christ himself in a new way. Not to recognise him thus is to throw a veil over the Old Testament or veil your own eyes so you do not understand that all that as an empirical institution was transitory; that the institution as such has ended and that covenant no longer has any sense as it was, because it has been superseded by the new covenant. Of course it did have a meaning, but its meaning was in its purpose, directed towards something else. Once the purpose has been achieved, the old covenant has fulfilled its mission.

Paul's play of ideas may seem difficult, but it is perfectly comprehensible in its logic of images and symbols. The apostle and Christians proceed in a very different manner, in a law of liberty and clarity, without veils, being totally exposed to the Spirit's shining. In verse 16 Paul quotes Exodus in the Septuagint translation: "but when a man turns to the Lord the veil is removed." The original is in the past tense: " but when he turned to the Lord", that is, when he went towards the tent of meeting, he took off the veil. Paul makes it future tense: "when he turns to the Lord he will take off the veil," because now it will not be needed. Who is the Lord for Paul? "The Lord is the Spirit." Moses turned towards the Spirit without veil, and so does the apostle. Christians must also do so when they receive the apostolic mission to spread the gospel.

"Where the Spirit of the Lord is, there is freedom." The new covenant is not a rule of written law imposing restraints, but a new rule of freedom of the children of God. "For freedom Christ has set us free" (Gal 5:1). This is a new central theme of Paul's message opposing the rule of the law to the rule of the Spirit. The freedom meant here is not purely arbitrary. Paul is not proposing the alternative *either law or license*, and to say so is doing him a grave injustice. The alternative is *either law or Spirit*, taking into account that the Spirit is more demanding than the law. The difference is that the Spirit demands but at the same time gives the strength to fulfil its demands. This is by way of parenthesis to stress the meaning of the phrase "where there is Spirit there is freedom".

Now we come to the final consequence: "And we all, with unveiled faces..." The singular has become plural. This is not a royal "we". Paul is speaking in a literal plural because he wishes to share his apostolic mission with the whole community, because it is up to the whole community to make the gospel present in word and life. The whole community has an apostolic mission, although the apostle Paul has been chosen in a special and extraordinary way to be the mediator of the gospel and agent of the Spirit. This could be called a democratization of the apostolate, because it is a task incumbent on all the people of God. People in Greek is *laos* and the adjective is *laikos*. A member of the laity is someone who belongs to the people of God. But although the apostolate is democratized, this does not mean that all have the same function. The people cannot occupy Paul's post, but they share something important with him, the mission to make the gospel present and they must do this – we stress once more – by word and above all by their lives.

Both the apostle and we other Christians must draw near to the Spirit and expose ourselves to him in order to *contemplate*. Contemplate does not mean poking or fishing about, but opening our eyes wide with astonishment to allow light to pour into us and impregnate us with new vision. It does not mean our capturing something but letting ourselves be captured and inundated. That is contemplation. For which it is necessary to take off the veil. We have to approach the Spirit and God's word open-faced and we reflect a glory which is not ours. The glory is from the Lord. We are not our own source of luminousness. We have been penetrated in contemplation by the glory of the Lord and then it breaks out from within us with a shining that is a reflection of this glory of the Lord, who is Spirit and Father and Messiah. When we are exposed in the contemplation of that glory we are gradually transformed into its image with growing splendour. The more we shine and the more energy we are – energy more than matter – the more we become like God who is light without form.

We were created in God's image. The image has been disturbed, spoilt and deformed. We have to recover this image, which has become full and revealed in Jesus. He was all shining of God the Father's love among us. He gives us his Spirit so that we are transformed from within. When we contemplate the Old Testament without veils as a manifestation in symbols of Christ's mystery, and when we contemplate the life of Jesus himself in the Gospel, we are not just assimilating something but assimilating ourselves to it. We become sources of reflected light from another glorious light. And this is not just a single definitive act; it is a process: "we are being changed into his likeness from one degree of glory to another." And he concludes "For this comes from the Lord who is the Spirit".

Before coming to an end we must stress the new character of contemplation. The written word of the Old Testament and the Gospel has to become a new text book for contemplation. We have to take off every veil of prejudice and worry to expose ourselves directly to Christ's life, which progressively unveils itself to us in the great Old Testament symbols and becomes fully present in the Gospel. When we are thus exposed to this shining we allow ourselves to be systematically and democratically transformed. Contemplate him and you will be radiant. Yes, we shall be transformed. Bit by bit we shall be reproducing the Lord's image. This is what the great New Testament saints did. So did Francis, Ignatius, John of the Cross, great saints who were transformed and became fountains of light, the shining of the Gospel. This is not imposed by force or violence or political-military power. It is a presence, an assimilation, a shining. Contemplate him and you will be radiant. It is Moses and the glory.

GREGORY OF NYSSA:
THE MOUNTAIN AND THE CLOUD

The knowledge of God is a mountain steep indeed and difficult to climb – and the majority of people scarcely reach its base. If one were a Moses, he would ascend higher and hear the sound of trumpets which, as the text of the history says, becomes louder as one advances. For the preaching to the divine nature is truly a trumpet blast, which strikes the hearing, being already loud at the beginning but becoming yet louder at the end.

The Law and the Prophets trumpeted the divine mystery of the incarnation, but the first sounds were too weak to strike the disobedient ear. Therefore the Jews' deaf ears did not receive the sound of the trumpets. As the trumpets came closer, according to the text, they became louder. The last sounds, which came through the preaching of the Gospels, struck their ears, since the Spirit through his instruments sounds a noise more loudly ringing and makes a sound more vibrant in each succeeding spokesman. The instruments which ring out the Spirit's sound would be the Prophets and Apostles whose voice, as the Psalter says, goes out through all the earth and their message to the ends of the world.

What does it mean that Moses entered the darkness and saw God in it? What is now recounted seems somehow to be contradictory to the first theophany, for then the Divine was beheld in light but now he is seen in darkness. Let us not think that this is at variance with the sequence of things we have contemplated spiritually. Scripture teaches by this that religious knowledge comes at first to those who receive it as light. Therefore what is perceived to be contrary to religion is darkness, and the escape from darkness comes about when one participates in light. But as the mind progresses and, through an ever greater and more perfect diligence, comes to apprehend reality, as it approaches more nearly to contemplation, it sees more clearly what of the divine nature is uncontemplated.

121

For leaving behind everything that is observed, not only what sense comprehends but also what the intelligence thinks it sees, it keeps on penetrating deeper until by the intelligence's yearning for understanding it gains access to the invisible and the incomprehensible, and there it sees God. This is the true knowledge of what is sought; this is the seeing that consists in not seeing, because that which is sought transcends all knowledge, being separated on all sides by the incomprehensibility as by a kind of darkness.

Wherefore John the sublime, who penetrated into the luminous darkness says, No one has ever seen God, thus asserting that knowledge of the divine essence is unattainable not only by men but also by every intelligent creature. When therefore, Moses grew in knowledge, he declared that he had seen God in the darkness, that is, that he had then come to know that what is divine is beyond all knowledge and comprehension, for the text says, Moses approached the dark cloud where God was. What God? He who made darkness his hiding place, as David says, who also was initiated into the mysteries in the same inner sanctuary.

When Moses arrived there, he was taught by word what he had formerly learned from darkness, so that, I think, the doctrine on this matter might be made firmer for us for being testified to by the divine voice. The divine word at the beginning forbids that the Divine be likened to any of the things known by men, since every concept which comes from some comprehensible image by an approximate understanding and by guessing at the divine nature constitutes an idol of God and does not proclaim God.

For it seems to me that in another sense the heavenly trumpet becomes a teacher to the one ascending as he makes his way to what is not made with hands. For the wonderful harmony of the heavens proclaims the wisdom which shines forth in the creation and sets for the great glory of God through the things which are seen, in keeping with the statement, the heavens declare the glory of God. It becomes the loud sounding trumpet of clear and melodious teaching, as one of the Prophets says, the heavens trumpeted from above.

When he who has been purified and is sharp of hearing in his heart hears this sound (I am speaking of the knowledge of the divine power which comes from the contemplation of reality), he *is led by it to the place where his intelligence lets him slip in where God is. This is called darkness by the Scripture, which signifies, as I said, the unknown and unseen.*

Life of Moses 158-9; 162-5; 168-9
PG 44, 376-77; 379

THE MOUNTAIN AND THE CLOUD
FOOTNOTE TO GREGORY

In the mountain we breathe a purer air, we listen to the silence. Our horizon is broadened, we feel the air caressing us. Down below we have left traffic, noise and bustle. Up here we savour solitude, we become reconciled to ourselves and to nature. But let us not climb too high where our lungs cannot breathe, and sheer rock is dangerous.

Going up the mountain Moses goes to meet God. A mountain is like an effort by the earth to get nearer to heaven. The mountains freeze movements made over millennia by the earth's crust. Moses goes up alone, leaving the people down below him unaware. But he takes with him humanity's millennial desire: the desire to go up and get close to God. Is God closer to the mountain than the valley? We feel him closer, and that is what it is about. Height can be a symbol of divinity; mountain climbing can be an active symbol of spiritual ascent: "the ascent of Mount Carmel".

Entering the cloud. How often whorls of cloud lie about the peaks. Banks of cloud hang on crags and gather in mountain hollows. Or they slip lazily along its sides. Cloud hides and envelops. God who comes near the mountain hides in the cloud. This polarity symbolises the mystery of contemplation, intimate dealing with God. We draw near to God to enter into his mystery: God attracts us and raises us in order to envelop us. Going up God's mountain is not seeing him clearly, because there the cloud of mystery veils his presence. Entering into the cloud does not mean staying in the dark, because the mountain broadens our horizon. The mountain teaches us to look from above, with perspective and serentiy. What a lot of nagging tensions are resolved or harmonized when we see this way! The cloud teaches us to penetrate into the invisible of the divine and human; feel where we cannot see and share this dampness which one day will become fertile.

7

Retirement and death of Moses

Moses is of course one of the greatest figures in Israel's history. He stands at the beginning of Israel as a people, he is the great leader who leads this people out of slavery to freedom, to meeting with God and *towards* the promised land.

We stress the preposition towards on purpose. There is a bit of a paradox and a lot of mystery. His calling suggested that all his activity and the great epic would end in a glorious triumph. He would not just lead the people *towards* the promised land but *into* it. But in a dramatic moment for the people the *into* changes to *towards*. Will he be left at the border? Must he undergo personal tragedy after having shared the long march with the people? Retirement and death are two concepts that do not necessarily go together. In our modern day culture death tends to be pushed back and retirement brought forward. It has become an ordinary regular event which happens to almost everybody and which some people look forward to. Moses' retirement has a completely different significance, because it happens to him at the precise moment when he is about to turn over the page and write the final chapter of his great enterprise. He has not yet reached the frontier of the promised land, but he is on the march towards it after overcoming innumerable dangers, and now all that is required is to enter it. One of the great events on the laborious journey has just taken place, the highly significant Balaam episode which has remained fixed in the people's memory, because in it they have seen an obvious sign of God's power.

A foreign king has not summoned up the strength of his armies but – what is much worse – the underground or cosmic magic power of a specialist in witchcraft, Balaam the sorcerer. The threat of irrational black magic worked by a magician endowed with powers superior to those of an army, powers that are uncontrollable by common mortals and which kings take into their service, powers that so terrified the ancients have been subdued and dominated by the Lord. The sorcerer has turned prophet and only says what God wants him to say: witchcraft has become prophecy, cursing turned to blessing.

The episode is still fresh in the reader's mind because two stories of lesser importance, or at least of less narrative weight, have done nothing to efface it. These are the second census and the problem of the inheritance of daughters.

When the two dangers have been overcome a census is made of the Israelites before they set out to cross the Jordan. And as the community of Israel has to continue in history, some laws are given to provide for the inheritance of daughters. Naturally what we have here is a projection, legislation for later events given at this point in the rather disorganized narrative which is the book of Numbers.

1. The announcement

In these circumstances something unexpected and terrible happens, which falls from heaven like a hammer blow that would flatten anyone without Moses' courage and resilience. Quite simply, the great leader is told he is to be compelled to retire, soon to die, and the announcement is made as if it is a punishment:

> The Lord said to Moses, "Go up into this mountain of Abarim, and see the land which I have given to the people of Israel. And when you have seen it, you also shall be gathered to your people, as your brother Aaron was gathered, because you rebelled against my word in the wilderness of Zin during the strife of the congregation, to sanctify me at the waters before their eyes. (These are the waters of Meribah of Kadesh in the wilderness of Zin.)" (Num 27:12-14).

What is this moment like for Moses? It requires an almost impossible effort to identify psychologically with Moses, feel how he had lived and put his life into the enterprise with which he had been entrusted and experience the violent blow that has

126

come to shatter his dreams. The blow falls at the very moment when these dreams seem about to come true. Does this mean that God repents of the great enterprise and is going to abandon the people in the desert? Or does it mean that God rejects Moses his faithful servant? Moses' disappearance has a tragic greatness. Any retirement for reasons of health or legal reasons has a sadness to it, because it is an anticipation of death. Death may arrive in unexpected and violent form (a cerebral stroke, a heart attack...) or it may be announced beforehand (an incurable cancer...). But retirement can also take the bureaucratic form of some years of service, which come to an end and further years – we do not know how many – which still remain. It is the final act, and all that remains is to wait for the curtain to fall. This is the context in which to set the retirement and death of Moses.

Moses was chosen to carry out a great enterprise, which he accepted and set going against his will. He resisted God as much as possible, but in the end he had to give in and accept. Now that he has carried out three quarters of this difficult task, he finds with surprise that God is forcibly retiring him. Isn't God contradicting himself? Because at the moment of his calling he said: "I am going to come down, I am sending you to bring this people out and take them to the promised land".

That is Moses' calling. He accepted it through obedience and has put all his soul into carrying it through faithfully, overcoming difficulties and bitterness. This man is impetuous and passionate. He has been educated in the Egyptian court and has proved to be a man of vision and talent. But if he has these qualities it is because God has given them to him to carry out the mission for which he was destined. Moses receives the mission and it is God's strength which launches it, making use of Moses as an energy source. It is as if a star, attracted or driven by a cosmic force, should feel that force within it as its own energy.

The same thing happens with Moses. He deployed enormous energy through having received his mission as an impulse from God's powerful hand. He could have remained in peace in a quiet life, as a father of children and husband of Zipporah, in Midian, with his father-in-law Jethro, the priest, but he did not. He gave up this tranquillity and took on the mission God had given him. And in the course of carrying it out he became identified with it. The same thing happens to us in our lives. We begin without much conviction, with difficulty, feeling lazy, we get into one chapter and we like it; a second chapter attracts us, a third leaves us enthusiastic and a fourth... Now we cannot disengage from the enterprise. It is this mysterious identification between the doer and the work, much more so if the enterprise is noble and the person engaged in it is large-spirited.

When he reaches this moment in history, Moses has stopped being himself and has become *his work*, with which he has identified totally. He lives and breathes for it and from it he appears to draw his strength. When the task is difficult, when there are problems to be overcome, then – like a difficult labour – it makes us love the work all the more, as if it were a child of our pain. What a lot Moses had to suffer! He had to endure the external hostilities of nature in the desert: hunger, thirst, serpents, the enemies who attacked this group of Bedouins, nomads travelling through the desert. Above all he had to suffer the hostility of his own rebellious people, grumbling, discontented, always asking for things and always dissatisfied; no sooner do they get one thing than they ask for another. Moses had to overcome all this with patience and dedication. But every victory, every pain accepted and overcome, is a progressive identification of himself with the enterprise, becoming it, embodying it as if it were flesh of his flesh. At this time does he not have merits to his credit which would allow him to complete in the joy of glory what he began one day in anxiety and foreboding of an uncertain future? No. At this moment he receives a categorical communication from God. It is not a threat, if you do this... if you don't do it. It happens simply like receiving a note in which a superior authority communicates an order already given: Retire and you are going to die. And what makes the communication even more tragic: death will come as a punishment for a sin.

Is it that Moses was incapable of responding to God's mission or did not use all his strength in the task? What was Moses' sin? Specifically, we do not know what this sin was. Perhaps a pious hand tore out the page which explained Moses' and Aaron's sin. But even if we do not know it specifically, we do know it in general: the sin of Moses and Aaron is that "you rebelled against my word in the wilderness of Zin during the strife of the congregation, to sanctify me at the waters before their eyes".

When the water failed the people protested, they wanted to quarrel with God, square with him as if demanding an account from him of everything he did. At that moment when it was a question of seeing God was right or not, Aaron and Moses weakened and did not fulfil the great precept to sanctify God's name and accept the mystery of his sovereign will; they committed the sin of wanting to know too much, not accepting, even rejecting, what God had done.

God's holiness is above all human calculation and understanding. Moses knew this holiness which was revealed from the beginning in an inaccessible fire on Mount Sinai. Moses had felt God's holiness near him in his life of prayer. At that moment he was not able to stand beside God in the dark of the mystery, he was unable to enter the cloud which hides and reveals God at the same time, he did not sanctify his name. For this he is going to receive death as a punishment.

A retirement because he was tired, worn out, to make way for another would have been very different. But he is retired as a punishment for something he did not do, and the rest of what he has done will be buried because of this sin. In the Lord's balance does one sin weigh more than so many sacrifices? But in this too God's holiness is revealed, even though it is difficult to understand. Moses must learn to accept that retirement coincides with a premature death – not in biological terms – a text tells us he was more than a hundred years old – but in terms of his task: he has not finished it.

He is ordered to retire from the task and from life. "You shall be gathered to your people." This is one of the many biblical euphemisms referring to death. Other texts speaks of a place where all mortals are given an appointment, and it is the world or kingdom of death. Mortals live scattered in time and space, perhaps at the same time but in a different space and they do not come across each other or meet. In the kingdom of the dead all mortals are given an appointment so that all are equal. In death everyone is "one more" who is going to be gathered to his people. Moses, like Aaron and the rest who went before them, suffer the same fate, with nothing special about it except that they are to die as a punishment for a sin committed in the desert at the waters of Meribah. It was a rebellion, a confrontation between the people and God – Meribah means quarrel, dispute

– and Moses on that occasion did not manage jealously to defend God's rights and holiness. God's confidant has to accept death as a capital penalty for that sin. That is how demanding God's holiness is!

2. Reactions

How does Moses react? In an ambiguous and complex way. We can study him in two texts that tell us about this reaction:

> And I besought the Lord at that time, saying, 'O Lord God, thou hast only begun to show thy servant thy greatness and thy mighty hand; for what god is there in heaven or on earth who can do such works and mighty acts as thine? Let me go over, I pray, and see the good land beyond the Jordan, that goodly hill country, and Lebanon' (Dt 3:23-28).

It is an emotional reaction, like a child's whose father forbids him something and the child pleads tearfully: Let me, please! The words reveal Moses' intense pain. It is neither protest nor rebellion against God's decision; it is a loving complaint divided into three parts. The first is: Lord, you have begun to show your servant your greatness and your mighty hand. I began by defending my brother in Egypt and I failed; I began by taking a wife and living a family life but you launched me on this enterprise. If you have begun and continued, you must finish it. But may not I who have begun and continued also finish it? If you began through me, finish through me too. You must be consistent with yourself, Lord. Let it not be said that you deceived me at the beginning or you have grown tired of me. You know very well how I am and, if one day I failed your holiness, now I confess that there is no one like you who can work such wonders as you have. Through this humble confession, Lord, forgive my sin when I did not sanctify your name and let me come into this land of fertile valleys and high mountains. I am tired of wandering through the desert and I want to rest. When I have the spiritual satisfaction of having finished the task, then, Lord, call me to my final rest.

This is Moses' prayer in chapter 3 of Deuteronomy. But the book of Numbers gives us a different reaction:

Moses said to the Lord: "Let the Lord, the God of the spirits of all flesh appoint a man over the congregation, who shall go out before them and come in before them, who shall lead them out and bring them in; that the congregation of the Lord may not be as sheep which have no shepherd" (Num 27: 15-17).

Here Moses is not thinking of himself; he only thinks of his people. Do these two versions contradict each other? In a critical analysis we would say that the two texts represent versions belonging to two different traditions, one collected in Deuteronomy and the other in the book of Numbers. As the traditions are different they focus on different things. According to one, Moses wept and begged not to be punished; according to the other Moses forgets about himself to pray that the enterprise might not come to nothing. This is a legitimate explanation. But we are interested in co-ordinating the two, in order to derive a deeper meaning from this synthesis.

The psychological response would be to say that Moses feels both things: he feels the pain of having to retire before finishing his work, with all the aggravating factors of the inconsistency of God's behaviour, as he withdraws his favour; and on the other hand he feels the enterprise is more important and above personal interests and feelings. In other words there is a conflict within Moses: there is his personal interest, his desire to finish the task and then enjoy the resulting tranquillity; and there is his concern that the people should not lack a leader who can continue his work. As well as two external narratives, there are two contrary and complementary internal forces tearing Moses apart and displaying his greatness of spirit and genuine humanism. Moses is revealed as one of us: we are not all of a piece, we do not act from a single motive, we do not judge by one measure. Different forces operate at once and battle it out for our minds and hearts. We fluctuate between personal interest and our duty to others. Both versions reflect the inner tension racking Moses. Deuteronomy reflects an emotional, intensely human moment, an understandable reaction, while Numbers brings out the gigantic stature of this man: I accept retirement but I pray that the work may go on.

"Lord of the spirits of all flesh": this title is found twice in the

Bible. The first time is in the episode of Korah's rebellion seeking power and opposing Moses' fundamental privileges. In the present complex case Moses prays as follows: "O God, the God of the spirits of all flesh, shall one man sin, and will you be angry with all ? It is you who gives life to each and every one of the living, because the mystery of life does not spring from matter without your strength, but is like a sharing in your life, which you generously communicate, while still keeping your sovereignty. You make one generation arise and another disappear from on earth, and you go on being the Lord of the spirits of all the living, especially living humans and also of all their gifts and talents. Each one receives a mission from you and the capacity to carry it out, and you know our gifts well and the capacities of each one of us. Therefore name a leader for the community to go in and come out in front of them, now that I have to retire from this mission that you yourself entrusted me with."

"Go out and come in" in Hebrew means the whole of human activity. The peasant goes out of his house, out of the city in the morning to work till evening (Ps 104) when, with his work done, he comes back into the city and his house to rest with his family. Going out and coming in represents the course of his activity, it is taking on and leaving off, beginning and ending. It is an expression that rhetoricians call *polar*, because with two poles it embraces a whole. It is equivalent to: until his death. Moses was free to carry out his work without being subject to anything or anyone else. Now he is going and it is for the Lord to appoint a new leader to take his place in these same functions. Between the two of them they will have done the work of going out of Egypt and coming into the promised land.

3. The successor

And the Lord said to Moses: "Take Joshua the son of Nun, a man in whom is the spirit, and lay your hand upon him; cause him to stand before Eleazar the priest and all the congregation, and you shall commission him in their sight. You shall invest him with some of your authority, that all the congregation of the people of Israel may obey. And he shall stand before Eleazar the priest, who shall inquire for him by the judgment of the Urim before the Lord; and at his word they shall come in, both he and all the people of Israel with him, the whole congregation" (Num 27:18-21).

Joshua is the successor chosen by God. He is a man of great qualities, with gifts of leadership, with the spirit of God, and he is consecrated in a liturgical ceremony. His qualities precede his election and consecration. Contrary to this, in the last chapter of Deuteronomy we hear of the imposition of hands and the coming of the Spirit as an effect of this imposition. Should we speak of a contradiction between these two texts? Again an analytical exegesis would say that here we have two different versions of the same episode. We say this is a legitimate explanation but that we prefer to take the text as it stands: Joshua already has the Spirit and the qualities, he has been acquiring them in his work with Moses, he has shown them in his role as assistant; but now, through the imposition of hands he still receives the Urim and is subject to God, although not in the same way as Moses. Moses went to the tent of meeting and spoke there with God face to face to receive the instructions which he then transmitted to the people. Joshua will not enjoy this unique privilege. As well as carrying the burden of a large body of precise general instructions, he will be dependent for many particular decisions on God's answer, not given directly but through the high priest, the administrator of the Urim. This is God's commandment which is to be obeyed:

And Moses did as the Lord commanded him; he took Joshua and caused him to stand before Eleazar the priest and the whole congregation, and he laid his hands upon him, and commissioned him as the Lord directed through Moses (Num 27:22-23).

This text can be filled out with another from Deuteronomy:

And the Lord said to Moses, "Behold the days approach when you must die; call Joshua, and present yourselves in the tent of meeting, that I may commission him." And Moses and Joshua went and presented themselves in the tent of meeting. And the Lord appeared in the tent in a pillar of cloud; and the pillar of cloud stood by the door of the tent (Dt 31:14-16).

133

We are given a further detail: the congregation stays outside God's presence in the cloud. The cloud is God's veiled presence; it says that God is present, but does not let him be seen. It suggests a presence but does not show it. Thus it veils and unveils at the same time; it unveils the fact without unveiling the form.

In the passage quoted above we read: "Commission Joshua, infuse him with courage and bravery, because he will go out in front of this people and will divide the land that you can see among them." Here we have the fresh detail of courage and bravery. Courage and bravery are necessary as well as knowledge and wisdom because the enterprise which has almost been concluded by Moses still presents many difficulties requiring valour. Moses will give him these in word and example, perhaps the best one being the dignity with which he retires. Joshua has lived at Moses' side as his assistant, he knows him and admires him, but perhaps there is much more to admire in the manner in which Moses retires. In the face of this greatness he will be filled with courage himself. In Deuteronomy 34 we are told that Joshua possesses great qualities, because Moses had laid hands on him. The Israelites obeyed him and did what the Lord had commanded Moses.

So this intermediate and necessary stage comes to an end: the measures Moses had to take to appoint and consecrate a successor before retiring and disappearing.

The final act: you will see it but you will not experience it. Before he dies, as a farewell to life and his task, the Lord invites Moses to go up a high mountain in the country of Moab to look down on the promised land. But first we have to go up a narrative mountain to be present at the act of transfer of power and liturgical consecration of Joshua. By this act the natural qualities he already had are reinforced and he will receive other new ones. Up till now he has never been a leader. All his work was in helping Moses as his assistant, and he had not received the Spirit he possessed as a share in Moses' spirit. In the episode in chapter 11 of the book of Numbers, Moses' spirit passed to the seventy elders. Now it is Joshua's turn to have his appointment as leader ratified by a liturgical act. The high priest will officiate before the community who accept him and approve him. The same thing happens as at a wedding where the guests are present but two people are the witnesses representing the whole community, the whole Church. Thus the whole community participates, giving legal sanction to a ceremony which contains the ritual of laying on of hands, transmitting a burden of power and prestige upon the head of the consecrated.

Is this enough to consider Joshua Moses' successor with full power? Yes and no. Joshua will occupy Moses' place, but he will not have all his powers. The priest Eleazar will consult the Lord for him by means of the Urim, and in accordance with the results of the oracle he and the whole community will come in and go out. Eleazar is the highest minister of the cult, but not the supreme religious authority, who is Moses, invested by God. When there is a need to take particular decisions not foreseen in the general instructions, it will be necessary to consult God by means of the Urim and it is Eleazar who has the task of doing so. The Urim are in God's hands, it says in the book of Proverbs (16:33). Therefore the Urim can be an answer by God administered by the high priest and carried out by Joshua, who does not have full powers but is subject to the high priest.

When the ceremony is over the community has a new leader and the moment has come for us to assist at Moses' death.

4. The last look

The Lord said to Moses, "Go up into this mountain of Abarim, and see the land which I have given to the people of Israel, and when you have seen it, you also shall be gathered to your people" (Num 27:12).

In Deuteronomy 3:27 we are given more detail:

Go up to the top of Pisgah, and lift up your eyes westward and northward and southward and eastward, and behold it with your eyes; for you shall not go over this Jordan.

And further on in another passage:

"Ascend this mountain of the Abarim, Mount Nebo, which is in the land of Moab, opposite Jericho; and view the land of

Canaan, which I give to the people of Israel for a possession; and die on the mountain" (Dt 32:49).

This is what he has still to do. The succession is all sorted out. Moses can die. He is ordered to go up the mountain to contemplate the splendid view from the top. With longing eyes dazzled by the desert light he is to contemplate in contrast the soothing sight of an undulating country of hills and valleys. It is like a vision of paradise God is offering the people. Going up to see the view from above is a marvellous experience, but going up the mountain to see and die, to see paradise without being able to enter it, is tragic.

Thus Abraham once went up (Gn 13) after Lot had contemplated and chosen the green and luxuriant plain of Jordan, while he had to stay up there. God also invited him to go up and view the whole promised land: it will be for your descendants. One descendant, Moses, will also look and hear God saying: "It will not be for you but for your descendants". Going up to look... Going up to die!

The Jordan geographically separates Canaan from Moab. It is a rather flat land with gentle hills, but near Jericho stands a fairly high mountain which has two names, Fasga and Nebo, although the latter is the most common. The mountain stands majestically to the right of Jordan like a curious person standing on tiptoe to gaze from the west at this land described as marvellous. Before him lies the vale of Jericho and then a mountain that slowly rises to its summit. On clear luminous days you can see the far off towers of Jerusalem. This is the Nebo in its geographical position. But the narrative goes beyond the merely geographical because Moses receives a highly important command from the Lord: Go up the mountain and look at the land. This is the last consolation, like the last request of a condemned man. Is it a blessing or punishment? Or perhaps both at once?

Moses had asked: Let me go in and see! And God answers: I shall let you see but not go in.

Lord, but seeing and not going in makes it doubly painful...!

And God: Yes, it is doubling the agony, draining the cup to the dregs. Let the last thing your eyes see before closing be the land I have promised you. Moses prepares to go up the mountain:

And Moses went up from the plains of Moab to Mount Nebo, to the top of Pisgah, which is opposite Jericho. And the Lord showed him all the land, Gilead as far as Dan, all Naphtali, the land of Ephraim and Manasseh, all the land of Judah as far as the Western Sea, the Negeb and the Plain, that is, the valley of Jericho, the city of palm trees, as far as Zoar (Dt 34:1-4).

Let us go up with him. Moses has been spiritually going up all his life. The summit of his life is Sinai. Now Mount Nebo will be the summit of his death. Between the two mountains stretches the huge triumphal arch of his prodigious history. Moses now goes up the mountain never to come down. He rises at every step, and when he reaches the top it seems he is on a giant pedestal, as if the mountain had risen under his feet so that he can look down. "The mountains rose, the valleys sank down to the place which thou didst appoint for them" (Ps 104). This mountain has risen because God has ordered it to, giving power to the earthly magma so that it rises at his command. He lowered the valley of Jordan and raised Mount Nebo. Why? So that Moses could stand high up and look down. What a magnificent pedestal for Moses to die on! The mountain stands opposite Jericho, at the gates of the promised land. And there God showed him all the land: in the physical impossibility we read that this is not just a literal gaze.

From there the pilgrim can distinguish with a telescope the high region of Jerusalem, sometimes to the top of Mount Ebal, the highest point in all Palestine. Moses looks east and west and north and south. His eyes sweep round. And the text names the region of Gilead, which is east of Jordan; Dan to the north; to the far north of Palestine lie Naphtali, Ephraim and Manasseh; southwards Judah stretches to the Western Sea – the Mediterranean – there sits Jerusalem. What God makes Moses see is beyond the scope of human eyes. By physical gaze and spiritual illumination God puts the promised land into Moses so that he can behold it. Looking at it is in a way taking possession of it according to ancient usage: looking over an unoccupied territory meant taking power over it. And God makes Moses' bodily and spiritual eyes pass over this promised land. When they see it his eyes, mind and heart are filled. As this or that detail of the land impresses itself, the shape of a valley, a mountain slope, his imagination expands and his heart enlarges until they are ready to burst. This is gazing before you die, or perhaps dying from having gazed.

God said: No mortal can see God and live, because God is too great for humanity. Perhaps the promised land is a bit like this? It is so great, so immense, that Moses cannot gaze at it without dying. It is Moses' last look. From the mountain top he has looked back over his whole history, he has gathered it in his memory and brought it to mind with a certain melancholy. Now his eyes are going to embrace the whole land, they are going to be filled before being closed for ever. But first he is to hear God's voice saying: "This is the land of which I swore to Abraham, to Isaac and to Jacob, 'I will give it to your descendants.' I have let you see it with your eyes but you shall not go over there" (34:4).

Moses gazes, ends his contemplation saturated with history and landscape and closes his eyes to open them never more. Mount Nebo is the pedestal of his life and death:

> So Moses the servant of the Lord died there in the land of Moab, according to the word of the Lord, and they buried him in the valley in the land of Moab opposite Bethpeor; but no man knows the place of his burial to this day (34:5-6).

This is Moses' last sacrifice: seeing that his work is not finished. But he dies with a hope: not only has he glimpsed geographically the other side of Jordan, the promised land, but he has also glimpsed the future that is coming. He dies suffering, but not frustrated. On the other side of Jordan he has seen the dawn of a new glorious history which is now beginning. In part it is he who has prepared it. He has been able to see the moment in which the page is turned over to begin a new and important chapter. With this security, his eyes fixed on the future, Moses closes his eyes for ever.

> Moses was a hundred and twenty years old when he died; his eye was not dim, nor his natural force abated. And the people of Israel wept for Moses in the plains of Moab for thirty days; then the days of weeping and mourning for Moses were ended.
>
> And there has not arisen a prophet since in Israel like

Moses, whom the Lord knew face to face, none like him for all the signs and the wonders which the Lord sent him to do in the land of Egypt, to Pharaoh and to all his servants and to all his land, and for all the mighty power and all the great and terrible deeds which Moses wrought in the sight of all Israel (Dt 34:7-8; 10-12).

This is the epitaph: no other prophet arose like Moses, he was a unique prophet. One day Elijah will come ... but no one like Moses.

5. Appendix

Let us complete our meditation on the death of Moses with an appendix. Some time before he had received strict prohibitions from God:

"When you come into the land which the Lord your God gives you, you shall not learn to follow the abominable practices of those nations. There shall not be found among you any one who burns his son or his daughter as an offering, any one who practises divination, a soothsayer, or an augur, or a sorcerer, or a charmer, or a medium, or a wizard, or a necromancer. For whoever does these things is an abomination to the Lord; and because of these abominable practices the Lord your God is driving them out before you" (Dt 18:9-12).

"The Lord your God will raise up for you a prophet like me from among you, from your brethren – him shall ye heed" (Dt 18:15).

What does this text mean? The Israelites cannot be like other peoples who resort to the irrational world of magic to plan their lives. The Israelites depend on the Lord's will, expressed in the law; and if the law, being general, is not enough, if individual circumstances of history confront them with new and difficult decisions, then they will have the word of the Lord transmitted by means of the prophet. God will make prophecy institutional, sending as and when he wishes prophets for various circumstances. Thus arose first Elijah, a new Moses who in the course of his life had to embody the law and make a journey to Sinai, the Lord's mountain, for a personal encounter with him. After him will come that series of prophets with the illustrious names we know and others who from anonymity have incorporated their texts in already existing works or have sheltered under famous names: Isaiah, Jeremiah, Ezekiel, Hosea, Micah, Jonah etc.

After the return from exile two prophets are still in action: Haggai and Zechariah. After that prophecy dies out. Does this mean that God does not fulfil what he has promised to his people and that they have to live on eschatological promises and apocalyptic visions?

In the first book of Maccabees we read of events taking place about a hundred and fifty years before Christ. After having fought the Greeks, whose capital is Antioch, they gain national independence and appoint a supreme leader with full powers in civil, religious and military affairs: he is called Simon and in chapter 14 we read of him:

> The Jews and priests are happy that Simon should, pending the advent of a genuine prophet, be their ethnarch and high priest for life (1 Mac 14:41).

This information is very important, because it means that all the acts of the Maccabees are made relative to God's disposal if God wants to send an accredited, genuine prophet to pass definitive judgment on the enterprise. However, a prophet like Moses, or one in the series of Isaiah, Jeremiah, and Ezekiel did not arise either then or in the years that followed. It was necessary to wait until a prophet arose or, more exactly, *The Prophet*, one of your own, a brother, a Jewish Israelite, and that prophet was Jesus. Chapter 18 of Deuteronomy points forward towards him: I will raise a prophet from among you, from among your brothers; him shall ye heed. Therefore the figure of Moses is a type, an example, pointing towards the figure of Christ. Christ too will have to go into the wilderness, he will have to go up Mount Tabor for his transfiguration and Mount Calvary for his death. When this prophet arrives who is not *a* word of God but *the Word* of God made flesh, at the moment of his transfiguration the great prophet Moses hears a voice calling. He who has slept for centuries now keeps the appointment, as in the past he went to the tent of meeting, for a new meeting which he never suspected in his lifetime. For on top of Mount Tabor, without artificial tents, in the visible reality of a human body, the glory of the Lord is present wanting to speak to people. Moses keeps this historic appointment from out of his sleep of centuries: beside the glorified Lord appear Moses and Elijah representing the law and the prophets. There, lit by the splendour of the Messiah, their historic work, their persons and their writings (or those which bear their names) are bathed in a new light, because it is the Lord. It is the new Moses, who will not give a law like the old one, but go up a mountain to give us the beatitudes. They are not commandments or prohibitions but formal guarantees of blessing: blessed are those who do this and that...

Moses died on Mount Nebo; Jesus died on Mount Calvary, also with his work half done, humanly frustrated. But Jesus also named his successor: the Spirit of the Father to finish his work, who is his own Spirit.

GREGORY OF NYSSA: DEATH OF MOSES

After all these things he went to the mountain of rest. He did not set foot on the land below for which the people were longing by reason of the promise. He who preferred to live by what flowed from above no longer tasted earthly food. But having come to the very top of the mountain he, like a good sculptor who has fashioned well the whole statue of his own life, did not simply bring his creation to an end but he placed the finishing touch on his work.

What does the history say about this? That Moses the servant of Yahweh died as Yahweh decreed, and no one has ever found his grace, his eyes were undimmed, and his face unimpaired. From this we learn that, when one has accomplished such noble actions, he is considered worthy of this sublime name, to be called servant of Yahweh, which is the same as saying that he is better than all others.

For he who elevates his life beyond earthly things through

141

such ascents never fails to become even loftier than he was until, as I think, like an eagle in all things his life may be seen above and beyond the cloud whirling around the ether of spiritual ascent.

Life of Moses 307
PG 44:425

COMMENTARY

Gregory sees the death of Moses as a completion, an ascension, a coronation. He completes his existence and mission, finishing what he has modelled, the statue of his life (for which the mountain will be a pedestal). He ascends to the top, to the height, towards God. He is crowned with a title that seals his activity: "servant of the Lord" (as if he were canonized). Thus Moses offers himself as a model of spiritual ascent for the Christian seeking perfection.

What more trustworthy witness of the fact that Moses did attain the perfection which was possible would be found than the divine voice which said to him: I have known you more than all others? It is also shown in the fact that he is named the friend of God by God himself, and by preferring to perish with all the rest if the Divine One did not through his good will forgive their errors, he stayed God's wrath against the Israelites. All such things are a clear testimony that the life of Moses did ascend the highest mount of perfection. Since the goal of the virtuous way of life was the very thing we have been seeking, and this goal has been found in what we have said, it only remains for us to transfer to our own lives what we have contemplated in the story so that God may choose us as friends. This is true perfection: not to avoid a wicked life because like slaves we servilely fear punishment, nor to do good because we hope for rewards, as if cashing in on the virtuous life by some business-like and contractual arrangement. On the contrary, disregarding all those things for which we hope and which have been reserved by promise, we regard falling from God's friendship as the only thing dreadful and we consider becoming God's friend the only thing

worthy of honour and desire. This, as I have said, is the
perfection of life. As your understanding is lifted up to what
is magnificent and divine, whatever you may find (and I know
full well that you will find many things) will most certainly be
for the common benefit in Christ Jesus. Amen.

Life of Moses 319-2
PG 44:429

COMMENTARY:

Gregory resumes all perfection in being "friends with God"
as a result of God's "choosing". Friendship with God has a
reciprocal character and must be sought above all things.
Moreover love of God has to be the single motive for our actions,
not fear of punishment or hope of reward. This is the theme of
the well-known hymn: "My God, I love thee, not because..."
And the conclusion lies in those other famous lines:*

Therefore with my utmost art
I will sing thee.
And the cream of all my heart
I will bring thee.

• By George Herbert.